THE LEADERSHIP OF TEAMS

THE LEADERSHIP OF TEAMS

How to develop and inspire high-performance teamwork

MIKE BRENT AND
FIONA ELSA DENT

Bloomsbury Business
An imprint of Bloomsbury Publishing Plc

B L O O M S B U R Y
LONDON • OXFORD • NEW YORK • NEW DELHI • SYDNEY

BLOOMSBURY and the Diana logo are trademarks of Bloomsbury Publishing Plc

First published 2017

British Library Cataloguing-in-Publication Data
A catalogue record for this book is available from the British Library.

ISBN: PB: 978-1-4729-3587-8
ePDF: 978-1-4729-3588-5
ePub: 978-1-4729-3589-2

Library of Congress Cataloging-in-Publication Data
Names: Brent, Mike, author. | Dent, Fiona Elsa, author.
Title: The leadership of teams : how to develop and inspire high-performance teamwork / by Mike Brent and Fiona Elsa Dent.
Description: London ; New York : Bloomsbury Business, 2017. | Includes bibliographical references and index.
Identifiers: LCCN 2017009700 (print) | LCCN 2017019945 (ebook) | ISBN 9781472935885 (ePDF) | ISBN 9781472935892 (ePub) | ISBN 9781472935861 (eXML) | ISBN 9781472935878 (pbk.)
Subjects: LCSH: Teams in the workplace–Management. | Leadership.
Classification: LCC HD66 (ebook) | LCC HD66 .B737 2017 (print) | DDC 658.4/092–dc23
LC record available at https://lccn.loc.gov/2017009700

Cover design by Sharon Mah
Cover image © Ivcandy/iStock

Typeset by Integra Software Services Pvt. Ltd.
Printed and bound in Great Britain

To our families

CONTENTS

ABOUT THE AUTHORS

Michael Brent is Professor of Practice and Adjunct Faculty at Ashridge Executive Education, Hult International Business School, one of the leading business schools in Europe. He specializes in leadership, team-building, influencing, coaching, cross-cultural management, leading change and personal development. He now also runs his own coaching, training and consultancy company and has a particular interest in working with management teams.

He has co-authored four other books on leadership with Fiona.

Mike believes the key aspects of leadership are self-awareness, and skill and flexibility in responding to others. Managers and leaders must operate in areas where there are many dilemmas and 'wicked' problems, and therefore must develop the ability of *not knowing* to go with their ability to make decisions.

Mike holds both British and French nationalities and is bilingual.

Fiona Elsa Dent is a Management Trainer, Leadership Coach and Professor of Practice at Ashridge Business School. Fiona now has a portfolio career having worked full-time for more than thirty-five years. She was a faculty member at Ashridge for twenty-four years and during her last ten years on the full-time staff she held a role on the management team as Director of Executive Education where she managed a faculty group and contributed to the strategic operation of the organization.

Fiona now enjoys a mixed portfolio of teaching, coaching, researching and writing. She still contributes to a variety of programmes at Ashridge and also works for a range of clients as a management trainer and coach. She enjoys researching and writing and since moving to a portfolio role has published three books in addition to this one: *The Leaders Guide to Managing People*, *The Leaders Guide to Coaching and Mentoring*, both with her co-author Mike Brent, and *How to Thrive and Survive as a Working Woman: The Coach Yourself Toolkit* with her co-author Viki Holton.

ACKNOWLEDGEMENTS

We would like to express our appreciation to all the managers who have over the years attended our leadership development programmes and been able to tell their leadership and team stories. We also wish to thank those who actively contributed to our thought processes in writing this book.

Our thanks go to Ian Bell, Alan Gentle, Alex Davda, Hans Friberg, Helena Gaunt, Helen Bailey, Francoise Nash, Mike Stonor, Stuart Green, Peter Hawkins, Viki Holton, Sue Honore, Tom Powers, Dr Mark Lowther, Dame Carolyn McCall, Dr Mark McKergow, Dominic Mahoney, Nigel Melville, Carina Paine Schofield, Will Shorten, Tamsin Simmons, Rolf, Christoph, Simon, Pierluigi, Gery, Jane, Feisal and Laurent from the 1st Host Leadership Conference and to Tony (Spreaders) Spreadbury and his team at the England Rugby Football Union.

Special thanks to Sharon West and Mike Dell for their support.

Introduction

In our work we hear the words 'teams' and 'teamwork' constantly, and we were struck by the fact that very few people in teams ever reflect on what exactly a team is, how it works or how it could work even better. What exactly *is* a team? And do we always need teams to do the work? Is there a difference between a team and a group?

So we decided to explore the world of teams and find out what they are, if and when they are necessary, and what could be learned about both leading and participating in teams. We looked at the research, called on our own experience of leading and working both in and for teams, observed teams and interviewed team leaders and members from a variety of different fields, including the business world, the arts, sport, the military and medicine.

Where does the word 'team' come from?

The word 'team' derives from the old English and Norse word for 'bridle', and from that came the meaning of a set of animals, harnessed together, which would pull ploughs to till the land. From this definition comes the analogy of people involved in joint action. The concept of 'team' must be one of the most commonly used ideas in organizational life. However, we think that it is overused, in the sense that many so-called teams are not in fact *real* teams.

A research report by Deloitte University Press (2016) stated that 'Businesses are reinventing themselves as networks of teams in order to keep pace with the challenges of a fluid unpredictable world.'

We believe that there is significant progress to be made in how teams work effectively, and that team leaders and team members can realize the full potential of effective teamwork. We hope that this book can contribute to this progress.

In our experience, working with many different types of teams across many businesses, organizations and countries, we have often found that the team leader had no specific training either in psychology or in team dynamics. They were often highly skilled individuals in their specific technical area, but lacking in the skills that would help them make the most of their teams' potential. We specifically found it disheartening when the so-called team leader did not involve or engage all the members of the team, or when the leader ignored contributions, or worse still, dismissed ideas as being rubbish. It's not enough just to have the title of team leader; we believe that there is a need for the leader to gain specific knowledge and training in order to unlock the team's full potential.

In this book, we offer a practical and comprehensive review of teams and teamwork. We discuss why effective teamwork is so important and also examine many different aspects of teams, team leadership and team membership. Some of what we offer are reminders about some of the well-known theories and models – such as team roles, team processes and stages of team development. We discuss how to deal with issues such as trust, engagement, conflict, politics and change in the team. We also give ideas on tools and techniques for team success, such as how to coach, influence and facilitate teams. We highlight the dangers of team members derailing and how to avoid it. Finally, we look at the future of teams – where we believe that all team members, not just the team leader, should be able to have the skills to lead the team effectively.

We hope that in addition to refreshing your knowledge of teams and team working, you will find some useful new ideas, tips and techniques. The book is designed so that you can dip in and out of it, and we hope that it will help you to become an even more effective team leader and team member.

1

Teams – what and why!

T – Together
E – Everyone
A – Achieves
M – More

What is a team?

The usual definition of a team is, 'A small group of people with complementary skills and a common purpose' (Katzenbach and Smith 1993). Small, because too many people and a team will be ineffective. The accepted range for an effective number of people in a team tends to be between five and twelve people, although Wharton Business School professor Jennifer Mueller concludes that six is optimal. Although important, the number of people is not as important as the quality of the people and the type of leadership demonstrated within the team. We suggest that teams work best when they have members who have complementary skills and approaches. Having people with different skills and preferences will help to gain the maximum amount of diversity to achieve the team goals and success. For the team to achieve anything, it should also have discussed and agreed its common purpose. It's actually quite amazing how many so-called teams exist which have not discussed the issue of complementarity or indeed defined any common purpose.

Researchers Jon Katzenbach and Douglas Smith made the useful distinction between working groups and teams. These are not the same thing and they have very different goals and objectives, need different skills and produce different results. Working groups, for example, share information, perspectives and insights. They place their focus on individual goals and accountabilities, and not on taking responsibility for results other than their own. Teams, however, will also focus on mutual accountability and responsibility. There are a number of other differences between working groups and teams. Teams, for example, have a specific team purpose as well as the more general organizational mission to follow. A group is likely to have a specific leader, whereas a team could have a nominated leader but is also able to share leadership roles.

The main thing to remember is that just because you call a group of people working together a team, that doesn't magically make them into one. Until you work to develop specific team attributes, it will simply be a working group. That said, effective working groups can sometimes be more productive than ineffective teams. But at their best, real teams will outperform working groups.

Some organizations persist in calling a bunch of people who happen to do some work together a team. We often see this in so-called management teams, when we are asked to come in and help them because they are behaving in a dysfunctional manner or simply not working together effectively. To create an effective team takes time and effort – it simply will not happen by chance. In this book, we will describe many ways of making your group into a team, or making an ineffective team into a better one.

LESSON FROM BUSINESS

We interviewed a team member from an award-winning business development team. The team won an organizational award for 'Client Focus' and it is multifunctional, multicultural and multigenerational. It also contributes towards the success of a wider business team within the organization.

On the topic of what makes the team a team rather than simply a group of people, the team member in question attributed it to a range of things:

- *Starting with the recruitment process – in which everyone is involved. The aim of this is to ensure that they all feel new people will fit with the culture of the team.*
- *On the whole, people in the team get along and all have a good sense of humour.*
- *The team structure is pretty flat and non-hierarchical, friendly and focused on business targets.*
- *Regular team meetings are an important feature of the team's success. All team members are involved in all meetings. Each meeting has a different purpose:*
    - *Regular Monday morning meeting*
    - *Strategy meeting*
    - *Social lunches to celebrate success, welcome new joiners, etc.*
    - *Sales pushes, where all team members get onto the phone to try to get leads*
    - *Weekly pipeline meetings*
- *This regular whole team communication has significantly contributed to the team's success and means that on the whole the team members are energetic, client-focused, responsive and committed to the client process.*

He feels that a key feature of the team is its driven and go-getting nature.

Why are teams important?

Good teamwork can enhance the performance of any organization. As the well-known American football coach and businessman Vince Lombardi said, 'Individual commitment to a group effort – that is what makes a team work, a company work, a society work, a civilization work'. We have identified a range of reasons why we believe effective teams and teamwork are important for success in today's organizational life; these are discussed below.

Our volatile, uncertain, complex and ambiguous world

We live in a so-called VUCA world, an acronym which was coined by the American military, meaning volatile, uncertain, complex and ambiguous.

- **Volatile** – The reality is we live in a turbulent world where situations are liable to change rapidly and unpredictably, often for the worse.
- **Uncertain** – The feeling of uncertainty is more pronounced than ever before, where it is less likely that future events can be predicted.
- **Complex** – Our world has become ever more multifaceted, which has led to increased difficulty in understanding.

- **Ambiguous** – Many of the issues we confront are capable of being understood in more than one way, and thus consensus is difficult to achieve and conflict becomes more likely.

It is therefore increasingly difficult for one person (no matter how brilliant or how high up the hierarchy) to have the answers to all the problems and dilemmas faced by our organizations.

Teams enable creativity and innovation

By their very nature teams are made up of different people with different personalities, perspectives, opinions, needs, etc. The key issue here is that this diversity must be leveraged in order for high performance, and true creativity and innovation to happen.

Dealing with 'Wicked Problems'

Team leaders also now have to address what Professors Horst Rittel and Melvin Weber (1973) called 'wicked problems'. Here 'wicked' doesn't mean evil, but rather resistance to resolution. The definition of a 'wicked' problem is that solutions to wicked problems are not right or wrong, but better or worse. In other words, there is no one single agreed right answer to the problem. More and more of the problems that leaders and teams face are of this kind, yet often the leader is expected to know the answer, when there is actually no answer – only options, ideas or possibilities. We cannot underestimate the pressure that leaders feel to find *the* answer, even when there is no single possible answer.

There are, of course, times when we still face less complex issues. These are issues which are fairly well known and where there is no uncertainty involved. These issues can be described as 'puzzles', and individuals can solve them, so when faced by puzzles team members can often act and decide alone. On the other hand, when faced with more complexity and less certainty, an issue can be described as either a complex problem that does have solutions, or as a dilemma that actually doesn't have any one single solution. When faced with this type of problem, we need to work together in teams in order to leverage diversity, seek different opinions and challenges, and see how we can use the collective intelligence of the team to find the best possible solution.

When faced with even greater uncertainty – or dilemmas – we still need to use a team, and must expect divergence, challenge, creativity and honesty at this level. This will ensure that the best possible outcomes are reached. There are no simple solutions at this level of complexity, but there is a need for team members to be able to speak truthfully and to challenge each others' thinking in order to fully explore the issue and be truly creative and innovative. So, when faced with such 'wicked' problems, the team needs to create options, alternatives and possibilities *before*

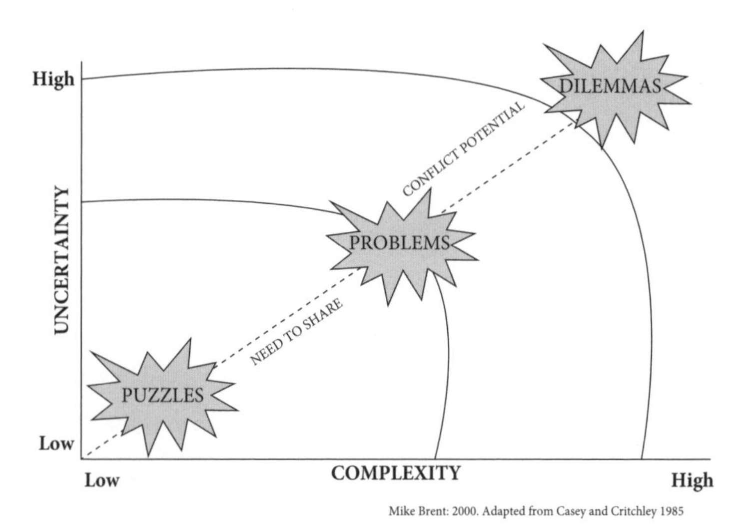

FIGURE 1.1 *Types of problems.*

they can decide on a particular course of action. See the diagram that follows for an illustration of this.

Teams facilitate learning and development

In a complex world, learning is critical and the opportunity for learning and development is boosted by effective teamwork. Our research into the working patterns and needs of the younger generation – the so-called Gen Y and Millennials, together with our research with managers in general – indicates that they want to work in environments where they can constantly learn and develop. To work effectively in today's complex and uncertain environments, learning must keep up with or exceed the rate of change.

Contemporary work is increasingly done in teams

Most things actually get done in teams. Our research at Ashridge shows that 69 per cent of managers work with five or more teams and that 88 per cent of the respondents were responsible for at least one team's performance. The research also identified that working and getting the best from a team wasn't an easy thing to do. It found that:

- The failure rate of complex teams is as high as 50 per cent.
- Only 12 per cent felt that their organization had good techniques to evaluate team performance.
- 98 per cent wanted a balance between task and process yet felt their organization wanted the task achieved at any price!

Work groups and teams are the backbone and lifeblood of most organizations, so developing effective team working processes and excellent team leaders are both critical areas for organizational success. It's worth investing time and energy into improving your way of working in and leading teams. In this book, our aim is to describe useful tools and techniques to help you create effective teams and to be an excellent leader of teams!

Key points from this chapter

- Effective work groups and teams are a key element of organizational life.
- Successful teams have diverse and complementary skills.
- Younger generations want to work with others in a collaborative way.
- 'Wicked problems' demand more collaboration.

2

Leadership and teams

You don't lead by pointing and telling people some place to go.
You lead by going to that place and making a case.

KEN KESEY, AUTHOR OF *ONE FLEW OVER THE CUCKOO'S NEST*

There are countless theories about how to lead a team, but it can be helpful to take a step back and look at the overall field of leadership for a moment.

Two metaphors that have been commonly used in team leadership are the leader as hero, and more recently the leader as servant (Greenleaf 1970). The hero typically is the boss who knows what he (or she) wants, has a clear sense of direction, doesn't really want to hear ideas from the team, and is not afraid to step forward and tell the team what to do. This seems to be quite a common occurrence in teams. But that of course is the extreme end. At the other end is the Servant Leader metaphor, and typically this leader would be stepping back, asking questions, observing and listening to the team members, who would see themselves as being in service to the team and the organization.

Reality more often than not lies somewhere along the spectrum, and is often messy and confused. Team members can speak but they are not listened to, or they are politely listened to but their ideas discarded. Or the leader listens and acts on ideas but then, if there are many different ideas coming from the team, which one to act upon?

Let's explore both of these metaphors in a bit more detail.

The leader as hero

The leader as hero is deeply ingrained in society, has proved itself as a stubborn metaphor and may be rather difficult to replace. Although it is now criticized, and seen as increasingly irrelevant in a VUCA world, it is, as Harvard scholar and writer Sharon Daloz Parks says, 'A deep and abiding myth' (Parks 2005, 201). Team members sometimes need to feel in safe hands and want a clear sense of direction.

So, if you have a heroic leader, where does that leave the members of the team? They might then be considered as victims or passive followers. That cannot work in a complex world where we need team members to be responsible, proactive and creative.

A good example of this is in the airlines industry. In the 1970s, there was a spate of accidents in the United States, where human error was found to be the case. The key factor in this human error was the key relationship between the pilots – that is between the Captain and First Officer. Many experienced pilots, and perhaps many who had served in the military, were quite autocratic in their behaviour. That meant that they thought they knew best, and consequently did not accept any challenges or feedback from their first officers, or indeed any of the crew. The term used by aircrew is 'cockpit gradient', and this refers to the difference in hierarchy between the Captain, First Officer and the rest of the crew on board. When the gradient is too steep, the First Officer is reluctant to oppose or challenge the Captain, even when he or she is fully aware that the Captain is making a fatal error.

As a response, the American Civil Aviation board brought in the concept of Crew Resource Management (CRM). The purpose of CRM training, which has been mandatory in Europe since 1997, is to improve teamwork in the cockpit, and therefore the safety of the aircraft, passengers and crew. Part of the CRM system is about being approachable, accepting feedback, involving all the crew and considering options. Teams outside the aviation industry, where there are also high consequences of failure, have started to use CRM. Again, we feel that this would be a worthwhile protocol to use in teams on the ground, even where the risks of failure might not be quite so dramatic.

LESSONS FROM AN AIRLINE

We interviewed an experienced pilot who captains aeroplanes for a leading UK airline. This is an extract from this interview.

Within the short-haul environment, the team on board an aircraft are different every day and often for each flight! Given that the Captain has overall responsibility for the safe conduct of the flight, it's vital for him or her to create an effective team ethic at the start of the day. During the pre-flight briefing an hour before the first flight, the Captain and First Officer will review the flight paperwork, and then introduce themselves to the Senior Cabin Crew Member (SCCM) and the other cabin crew in order to brief them on flight times, potential turbulence/weather issues, ATC delays and any relevant technical defects. It is at this point that the Captain can set the 'tone' of the day and certainly some Captains are better than others at achieving this important goal. The flight crew will also decide on which flights they will be acting as 'pilot flying' or 'pilot monitoring', considering the conditions on the day.

The intense nature of short haul operations, where there is very little time on the plane to maintain the team ethic, makes it extremely important for the Captain to walk to the back of the aircraft at each turn around to check on the crew's welfare and to determine if there are any issues. By doing this, the Captain can put him or herself in the crew's shoes and understand what is going on for them.

As this particular flight may be the first time the crew have operated together, it's vital that they are able to work as a team right from the outset. This is achieved by the implementation of very strict operating procedures for both the flight and cabin crew. In this way, an individual crew member will know what is expected of his or her colleagues in both routine and emergency situations, thus underlining the team element.

Furthermore, when faced with serious technical and emergency situations, flight crews will routinely use acronyms, such as DODAR, to guide their problem solving and decision making in order to achieve the safest possible outcome.

DODAR stands for:

***D**iagnose*
***O**ptions?*
***D**ecide/Do*
***A**ssign Tasks*
***R**eview*

Firstly, the flight crew will carefully 'diagnose' what the problem is, taking into account all the resources at their disposal, including information from the cabin crew. In fact, the cabin crew are actively encouraged to alert the flight crew to any problems or incidents. There is evidence that in one particular situation, the cabin crew heard an announcement by the Captain which they knew to be wrong, but they felt they could not challenge his authority.

Having diagnosed the problem, the flight crew will generate 'options'; whether to continue the flight, return to point of departure or divert. The Captain will then take the most appropriate course of action, having considered the opinion of his or her colleagues using open questioning such as 'what do you think?'.

With regard to 'assigning tasks', control of the aircraft is very often given to the First Officer, so that the Captain can better manage the situation, although the Captain will complete the landing, depending on the nature of the emergency.

Although airline procedures and processes are codified so that nothing is overlooked by the on-board crew, a key element of decision making within the cockpit is that all decisions should be reviewed. So even in an emergency where time is critical, the procedure demands a review.

In our opinion, this is perhaps something that teams in organizations would do well to follow. The key reason that a decision needs to be reviewed is that the situation can be very fluid and could change from one moment to the next. So if the situation changes, then the decisions taken might need to be changed as well to ensure a successful outcome.

Once the problem has been diagnosed, and an appropriate course of action taken, the flight crew use another acronym, NITS, to convey important information to the SCCM and Air Traffic Control. This means:

***N**ature of issue (brief description)*

***I**ntention? (continue, return to departure point or diversion to a suitable airfield)*

***T**imescale*

***S**pecial Instructions (preparation for emergency landing, if required)*

Importantly, the SCCM will be asked to read back the NITS so that misunderstanding is avoided.

The leader as servant

The idea of leader as servant was put forward some forty years ago as a deliberate counter to the flawed hero metaphor. Its main proponent was Robert Greenleaf in his book *Servant Leadership* 2002. It is attractive in many ways, in that the leaders' focus is on the needs of others, to listen to others perspectives, to support their needs and to involve them in decisions. But it also has its downsides, especially in certain cultures where hierarchy and position power are prevalent, and where leaders are expected to take responsibility and make decisions. Although the concept means that the leader should be in service to the organization, its employees and stakeholders, the metaphor of leader as servant is not entirely appropriate or relevant to our society. It can be off-putting to some groups of people and it hasn't really taken hold of the management community's imagination. It does, however, complement many of the other democratic leadership styles in that it can be regarded as a way of behaving rather than a style of leadership.

Host leadership

We believe that Dr Mark McKergow's (2015) concept of the leader as 'Host' is a useful way of helping leaders to resolve these issues. This metaphor offers a useful rethinking of both hero and servant leadership traditions. By building on both these ideas, it offers an interesting and relevant new way to conceptualize team leadership behaviours in the face of increasing complexity and change.

The act of hosting – receiving or entertaining guests or strangers – is as old as mankind. Hosts sometimes have to act heroically – stepping forward, planning, inviting, introducing and providing. They also act in service – stepping back, encouraging, giving space and joining in. The host can be seen encompassing aspects of both metaphors and the movement between them.

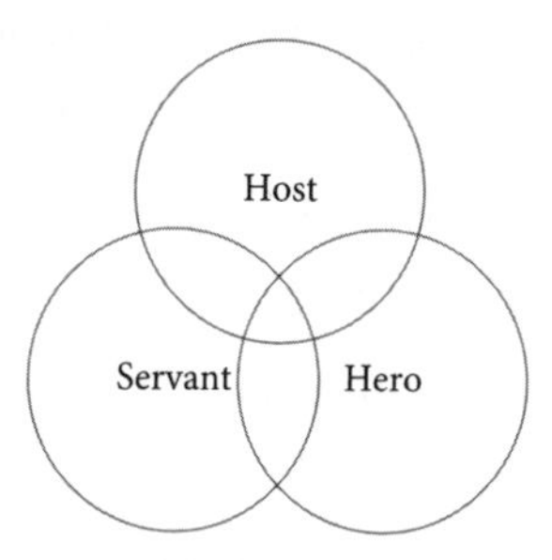

FIGURE 2.1 ***Implications of host leadership.***

There are several implications of host leadership. A leader as host would be:

- Relational – hosting can *only* happen with others (guests); in our example, the guests would be the team members.
- Invitational – hosts tend to use 'soft power' and a welcoming hand rather than coercion.

- Creating meaning – providing a context for new interactions and sense-making to occur.
- Thinking in phases – looking *around* the task and including preparation and reflection as integral activities.
- Taking care – the host has a traditional primary role in safeguarding their guests, and in this case it would mean taking care of the team and its needs.
- Taking responsibility – and therefore being accountable for what happens, whether planned or not. This implies that the team leader cannot just blame the team if things go wrong.

Stepping forwards and back

As host leader, you are alternating between stepping forwards (and acting somewhat heroically) and stepping back (serving, providing, leaving space open for others). To do this, the host leader needs three things:

- Awareness – of the spectrum of possibilities and how they connect with the organization and its work.

- Flexibility – to actually act and perform effectively in different places along the hero-servant spectrum.
- Timing – the contextual intelligence to know *when* to act, when to move, when to stand back and when to change tack.

Stepping forward – defining expectations

At the outset, it's your role as a team leader to gather people together and set expectations. You may want to help everyone to become clear about:

- What are the goals?
- What do you intend that each person brings to the table – skills, knowledge, etc …?
- What's important to you about *how* things will proceed? What expectations and boundaries will you put in place?

Here, you have stepped forward and set the frame. However, as you want to get the most out of your team, now is the time to step back a bit.

Stepping back – creating space for interaction

Once everyone is clear about your ideas, you are keen to give the team a chance to get involved. In CRM terms, this means using *all* the resources at your disposal. This doesn't mean being inactive – on the contrary, you will want to be alert and responsive. You can:

- Ask open questions to draw out people's expertise.
- Encourage discussion.
- Step back, listen and observe.

There might be a slow start... but hang in there. Give your team members a chance. You gathered these people together, and if you want to get the most out of them, you owe them the opportunity to get involved. It can be hard to open up a space for others to interact, and may feel a bit like losing control. But you are not losing control. On the contrary, you are still there, listening and engaged. And when the time comes, you can step forward again and nudge things back on track if you feel it's necessary.

When to step back and when to step forward? As a general rule, do one, then the other. If you want more involvement, step back a bit more often, and wait to see what happens. If things are moving too far off track, step forward and check that people are clear about what is expected and that you have a common understanding of what exactly is required. You will then develop a sense of how this works in your own team.

Applying host leadership – control versus letting go

How can host leadership usefully help in some of the dilemmas we mention above and help leaders to achieve better results in a more sustainable way? Let's look at a dilemma which particularly resonates with leaders in VUCA environments – control versus letting go.

Control versus letting go

At one end of the spectrum, there is dominating, being in control and having the answers; at the other end, relinquishing control, letting go, not having all the answers and allowing others to come up with ideas, and involving people in decisions which may have huge impact. If you are at the control end, there are certain advantages and disadvantages. If you are too much in control, then you are not delegating, not involving others in the team. Morale and commitment may suffer. But perhaps you feel that it's your job as a leader to be in control and to have the answers.

On the other hand, if you involve people too much, or give too much power away to the team, perhaps you would then feel that you are not leading. Others might ask what you are doing as a leader, if you are not coming up with the answers. Indeed, one of the many remarks we get from managers when we are leading coaching seminars is that their team expects them to lead from the front and give advice and help, not ask them what they think!

Let's consider how a host leader would approach this issue. The host puts in a lot of work up front. They figure out what they are aiming for, make preparations and invite people to join in. Even at this stage, they may be aiming to step back a little and involve others in the planning phases. They introduce people, make sure they have what they need, and *then* they step back, let things develop, while keeping an eye on what's going on. A host leader is always aware of their choices – to step forwards and nudge things along, or to make an active choice *not* to step forward right now but to see what emerges. The key elements are awareness and judgement. The leader as host will be aware of what's going on in the team, and make the decision to step forwards and intervene, or step back and allow things to develop, based on what is needed at that time.

If the leader *just* showed up and asked people what they thought, then the employees would be very justified in their dissatisfaction. That's stepping back without having stepped forward. And sometimes that is very difficult in certain situations, where there is a deeply ingrained culture of the leader being in charge and knowing the answers.

Sometimes, managers don't even have the awareness that these are two options. Let's see what happens when people spend all their time either stepping forwards or stepping back, without balancing their attention.

Dictator versus abdicator

We sometimes come across ***dictators*** – people who spend all their time laying down the law about what's to be done and how. You may have seen one or two yourself. They appear to have no time for anyone else's ideas or input. The ironic thing is that they are usually very committed to the success of their business – so much so that they are totally focused on doing things their way, in the mistaken belief that they, and only they, have the right answers.

Dictators can get success in the short run, but struggle to engage other people in a sustainable way. They tend to attract followers who like being told what to do – which is great for the short run but not a creative proposition for growing the enterprise.

On the other hand, we find the occasional ***abdicator*** manager too – someone who spends too much time stepping back and disengaging. This may be because they really don't care, but it is often because they think they have delegated something – and then don't check in, ask how things are going, or keep an eye out from a distance. In other words, they pretend to delegate but in actual fact they are dumping stuff on people.

So, a host leader would be both taking control and letting go – by mixing their actions in response to emerging events while keeping a wide awareness of both what's happening, how helpful it is, how to use their preparations for best effect and what else might happen *now*, at this moment in order to move things along. One key aspect of leading as a host is that anybody in the organization can act as a host. The role is not limited to the leader or senior management. In the case of a team, anyone in the team can assume the role of host and be proactive, rather than just wait for the team leader to take initiatives and make decisions.

Finally, be aware that if you wish to adopt this style of leadership, you are embarking on a journey that will take some time. You must work with your team to create a culture where host leadership is both understood and accepted.

LESSONS FROM BUSINESS

***Dame Carolyn McCall**, CEO of Easyjet and previously CEO at Guardian Media Group, tells us that in the past there was a definite command and control approach to leadership. She adds that there can be a time and a place for a directional and driven leader, and it can be effective in a crisis, for example, where you have to use your own judgement, don't consult and you take the decisions. However, Carolyn got more out of her staff at the Guardian newspaper, where she was the CEO, by coaching them on the issues they were facing rather than telling them what to* *do and how to do it. She strongly believes in a more coaching and developmental approach to leadership, and helping people to achieve their potential. This approach helps get and keep the right people, which you do not do with a command and control approach where there is no development. Executive development is critical and essential; if you don't have the right people, you can't achieve anything. As Carolyn puts it, 'One person can't change anything'.*

We also interviewed a team member *from a business development team who said, when asked about his team leader, that the leader used a coaching style of leadership where he asks questions, listens to others, gives people opportunities, gives credit and good feedback, and generally helps people to grow and develop. However, he also stated that when necessary the team leader could be assertive and provide direction. In addition, he also felt the leader was highly focused with good business and local knowledge.*

Key points from this chapter

- The team leader's job is to both step forward *and* to step back.
- Being stuck in either of these modes can be counterproductive.
- Host leadership is a timely and relevant concept for leading teams in complex times.

3

The stages of team development

Coming together is a beginning. Keeping together is progress. Working together is success.

HENRY FORD. FOUNDER OF THE FORD MOTOR COMPANY

Any team or group of people who work together will go through a variety of different development stages. Probably, one of the best-known models of stages of team development is Bruce Tuckman's model (which he developed when working with the US Navy). The four stages are Forming, Storming, Norming and Performing – to which he later added Adjourning. This model has stood the test of time and is really useful when working with teams and team leaders. It helps the team leader and team members if they can have open conversations about where they are in the development of the team, and what they can do to improve teamwork.

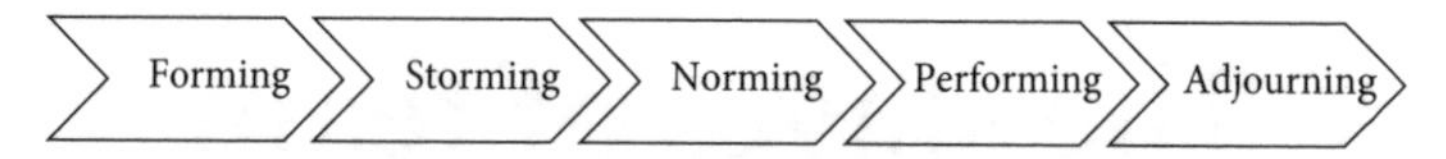

FIGURE 3.1 ***Tuckman's stages of team development.***

Let's look at each of these stages and explore what might be happening at each of the different stages:

Forming

This is when the group first forms, and as you might expect, it is characterized by hesitation in terms of how to approach both the task and the people. People will look for clear direction and may rush into task focus without thinking about team processes: that is, how they want to work together. Roles and responsibilities are not yet clear at this stage, and the leader's role is to reassure, explore people's motivations and preferences, and help team members get to know each other. It will also be important to launch a conversation to begin the exploration of the team's common purpose. Some possible questions to ask are: What is to be achieved? Why does the team exist? What are we here to do?

Storming

The next stage is one often characterized by conflict and jostling for position. Power becomes an issue, who has it and who doesn't? Cliques may form, leading to some people feeling a sense of belonging and others not. Emotions can run high. The team leader's job here is to leverage any conflict and work with it to help the team members understand purpose, roles, responsibilities and goals. This means conflict must be channelled in a constructive manner. There are two key dangers here:

- One is that conflict might be completely avoided and thus close down differences of opinions and idea generation, which would be a disaster for the team's creativity.
- The second is that conflict escalates, becomes personal and gets out of hand.

In either case, you then have a team which hasn't built mutual respect or trust, doesn't listen or communicate with each other, and is thus incapable of working effectively together. The team leader needs to ensure any differences of opinion are not personal and facilitate any conflict so that it is positive. For more about dealing with conflict, see Chapter 15.

One important tip while going through the storming stage is to remind the team of their common purpose and thus what they share. At each of these development stages, if purpose has not been established, it will make things very difficult.

Norming

Here, we now begin to see the formation of a more cohesive group. There is:

- clarification of roles and responsibilities
- goals become clearer
- harmony becomes important
- conflict and disagreement will be less evident
- discussions about team processes will take place
- people will begin to work together to focus on the task
- delegation within the group often happens here.

At this stage, one of the team leader's tasks is to create subgroups to ensure an effective working approach, where tasks can be delegated based on team members' preferences and skills. It will also be necessary for the team leader to ensure that any disagreement can surface so that the group doesn't fall into the trap of groupthink, where people are afraid to disagree and suggestions that could be useful are not voiced.

Performing

At this stage, the team is working well together, and the leader has established their own leadership approach. The team is tolerant of diversity, has a strategic awareness and has developed a common vision. Members have more flexibility and autonomy, and are able to actively help and support each other. The team leader will want to keep the team at this stage for as long as possible, although eventually the team's performance will drop off, unless it is constantly renewed. Achievements should be recognized and celebrated. There may be new members, so they will need to be properly integrated into the team. As team leader you need to promote and encourage diversity and make the case for it. Keep the big picture in mind and remind the team constantly of their purpose.

Adjourning

This is when the team breaks up, which is a natural part of any team's life cycle. It can be the end of the whole team or just some members leaving the team. The leader's role at this stage is to focus on two things – learning and appreciation. Anybody who is leaving the team should be properly thanked and recognized for their contributions. This is extremely important and often overlooked. It's then useful to go over what the team contributed to the organization, what the team members learned and how that learning can be fed back to the organization. This will mean that future teams can benefit and not have to reinvent the wheel. Finally, the team should celebrate together. This will help them move on, as there may well be a feeling of personal loss as the team breaks up. It also means that team members will then go into any new teams with a positive sense of energy and achievement.

This model is useful as it raises awareness that teams do actually go through different stages. It means that you as team leader can pay attention to the stage of the team and then try to intervene to move it on. It can also be helpful to realize that it is normal for teams to go through a period of being wary, having conflict, developing rules and ways of behaving, and then finally achieving results. But there is a danger in thinking that this is a straightforward linear process. When have you, as a team leader or team member, been part of a team that moved skilfully and seamlessly through these stages? Of course not! In reality, it is much, much messier than that. So we believe that it is more helpful to view the model as a dynamic process that sees the team forming, and going through storming, norming, performing and adjourning as a circular ongoing process.

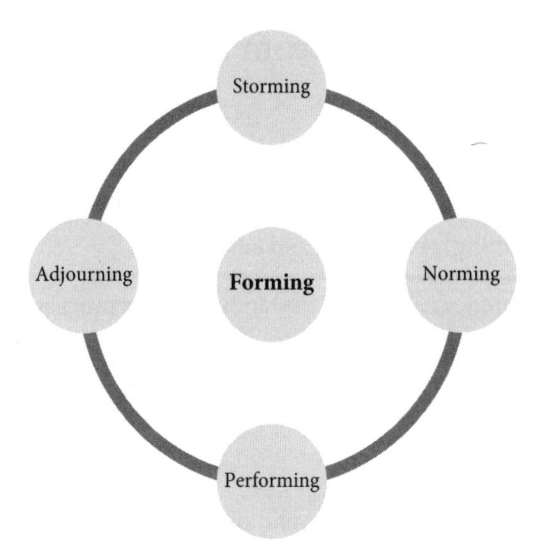

FIGURE 3.2 *The dynamic team forming process.*

Of course, the team would have to go through a reforming process when any new member arrived. When any new person joins, you must recognize that a process of integration is necessary. By this, we mean taking time to introduce the new team member to the other members, to the team's purpose and objectives, to the team's ways of working, and to their own role and responsibilities. We find that a buddy or mentor system works well, where an existing team member takes responsibility for the initial engagement and onboarding process.

Key points from this chapter

- All teams and work groups go through a rather predictable development process of forming, storming, norming, performing and adjourning.
- Awareness of and understanding of this process will help you to become a better team leader and team member.
- There are clear tasks to be paid attention to during each stage of the process.
- The process is ongoing and dynamic.

4

Team roles

Teams perform best when its members are fulfilling roles that appeal to them. In order for teams to be effective and to ensure the best performance, you will need to have an understanding of individual roles and appreciate how you as a leader can best apply the team role theories. A knowledge of the most popular team role theories will be useful. This will also help you to understand and identify your team members' role preferences, while ensuring they have the opportunity to perform to their best ability.

However, it is also important that team members recognize that it is not always possible to generate roles that appeal to them. On many occasions, in order to meet team objectives and outcomes, team members must be adaptable and willing to take on roles that contribute to the teams' success rather than simply their own preferences. Willingness to do so will serve both the team and the members well, and will act as a powerful development opportunity for all concerned.

When considering the roles that need to be fulfilled within a team, and in order for the team and its members to perform to their best ability, there are three areas to consider:

- The organization, its purpose and culture.
- The purpose of the team and its objectives.
- The team members.

Having clarity about the purpose of the team will enable you to think about the type of people and the roles required. In Chapter 5, we look at a variety of different team types and of course the purpose of any team will also be affected by the purpose, culture and values of the organization within which it operates. For instance, some teams are long-term teams and their key purpose is to fulfil their departmental business requirements. In this type of team, the participants will have a clear understanding of their day-to-day duties and responsibilities and will probably be performance-measured against these. Team members in these instances are often recruited against a set of criteria to ensure they have the required attitude, skills and abilities to fulfil their role. Other teams are created for a specific purpose, perhaps to meet a short-term requirement within a business, or to undertake a specific project. This type of team may require a different set of skills and abilities to the longer-term type team that operates on a more day-to-day basis. In short-term teams, the members may have to be willing to adapt and flex their role for the period of the teams' life in order to meet their objectives.

Team roles are often discussed in relation to an individual's particular behavioural preferences and skills: for instance, their preference for action, detail or creativity. We believe that good leaders and their high-performance team members will be far more successful if they are aware of these preferences. They also must consider the actual work of the team within the organizational context and then relate the purpose and the people to the roles, rather than simply allocating a person into a team.

Team role theories

Let's delve a bit further into the idea of team roles. Dr Meredith Belbin and his team at Henley Management College developed one of the most popular team role theories in the 1970s. Many managers and leaders will have come across this theory and most probably have completed the questionnaire that helps to identify their particular role preference when working in teams. Belbin's work contributed much to the understanding of teams and how they operate; his work is enduring and continues to be a useful and valid theory to help teams perform to their best ability.

Belbin initially identified eight team roles:

- Plant – the ideas person who is a creative and imaginative problem solver.
- Monitor Evaluator – the strategic thinker who explores options in depth.
- Coordinator – the orchestrator who brings people together to discuss and share ideas.
- Resource Investigator – the outgoing and communicative networker who enthusiastically develops relationships and opportunities.
- Implementer – the practical and reliable individual who wants to fulfil actions in a structured way.
- Completer Finisher – the conscientious and thorough individual who gets things done on time.
- Teamworkers – the caring person who operates well with others in service of a cooperative outcome.
- Shapers – the dynamic and challenging operator who is willing to confront issues to reach effective outcomes.

He then added a ninth role at a later stage:

- Specialist – the individual who adds expert skills and knowledge.

You could find out more about Belbin and his work and identify your own preferences by taking the Belbin team role questionnaire. You can also go to www.belbin.com to develop your understanding of how this can help you to fulfil your potential in any team, or read Belbin's book *Management Teams: Why They Succeed or Fail.*

Another popular team role model is one developed by Charles Margerison and Dick McCann, who created the 'The Team Management Profile' which identifies eight team role preferences:

- Creator Innovator – the creative one who comes up with new ideas and ways of doing things.
- Explorer Promoter – investigates possibilities and seeks new opportunities.
- Assessor Developer – the analyst who turns ideas into action.
- Thruster Organizer – keeps people on track to get results.
- Concluder Producer – works methodically to reach successful outcomes.

- Controller Inspector – takes a detailed view and control of the goals and objectives.
- Upholder Maintainer – ensures team performance by adhering to agreed values and standards.
- Reporter Advisor – gives and collects information.

Margerison and McCann also identified a ninth role for which they believed that all team members must take responsibility and this is called the 'Linker'. This role works to involve everyone who may be necessary in achieving success for the team. For more information about this theory and the Team Management Profile, go to their website at: www.tmsdi.com or read their book *Team Management: Practical New Approaches*.

Both the Belbin and the Margerison and McCann theories are widely used. They both promote the idea that when people understand their preferences, and work in roles where their particular skill set and behavioural preferences are used, it enables greater motivation and competence to perform. It is also true that both theories suggest that people will have more than one preference – often a main preference backed by one or two related roles. In essence, this can help people to understand why they are more motivated to perform in certain roles and teams than in others.

Another perspective

In our experience we find that in many team situations you cannot simply rely on taking on a role that is relevant for your particular preference. We believe that knowing your role preference is worthwhile and useful, but you also have to be flexible in order to fit into and perform effectively in teams. Moreover, people are frequently required to hold multiple roles in multiple teams, and while an understanding of your role preference can help you to take on duties that appeal to you, and that you are probably good at, you will also have to be adaptable and willing to flex the roles that you fulfil.

We offer you a slightly different approach in that we see six different role categories. We believe that, together with a knowledge of your team preference, these six orientations cover the main functions required to ensure that the team is able to perform its duties and meet its objectives. As a team leader, using this categorization can help you to allocate responsibilities (and possibly team roles) to the people who you believe will be best suited to undertake them. In each case, the orientation signposts the role requirements in a more general sense than either the Belbin or Margerison and McCann models do, and therefore may make them easier to apply on a day-to-day basis. Of course, these can also be used in conjunction with either of the other two approaches.

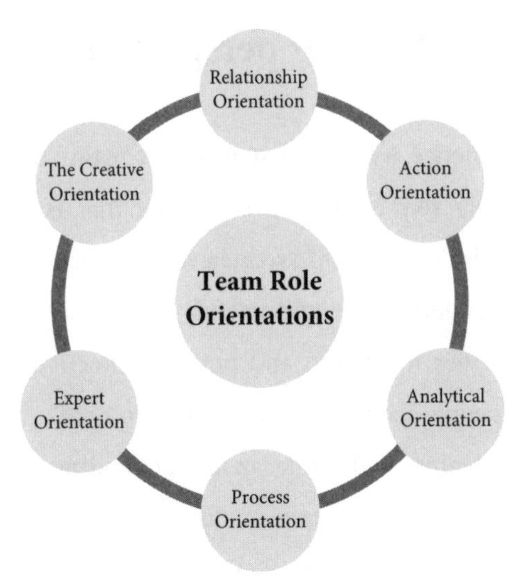

FIGURE 4.1 *Team role orientations.*

The relationship orientation

These are the people-oriented and social roles where team members have the abilities and inclinations towards encouraging, collaborating, listening and enabling others. This role often acts as a peacemaker, who regards their contribution as one of ensuring harmony within the team.

The action orientation

People who are achievement-oriented, energetic, task-focused, opinionated, persuasive and are keen to ensure that the teams' objectives are met and the job gets done. They can also be the people who want to take control and do things their way.

The analytical orientation

People taking this role have a desire to understand the rationale behind the issue the team is working on. They tend to want data and information to help them comprehend what is necessary, whether the objective is fact-based and achievable, or whether further research is necessary to fully appreciate the issue. These people ask detailed analytical questions, often requiring more work by team members.

The process orientation

Here, the individual wishes to understand the logistics and practicalities of how the group will achieve its objectives. They are concerned with meeting agendas, timings, who does what, action plans and deadlines. They will facilitate, coordinate and summarize to help people keep on track, will often point out the time and may even offer to make notes or take the minutes.

The expert orientation

Team working is not ideal for everyone, and there are always people in a network who can be regarded as 'experts' and who have a limited role to play in teams. Their main contribution is to bring their expertise to the team and the issue under discussion. Experts are often deep thinkers about their own area, but may be limited in their contribution overall. People with this orientation may tend to dip in and out of the team, as they are required, or possibly act as a specialist consultant to the team.

The creative orientation

This is the ideas person. They often encourage the team to look at things from new perspectives and suggest novel ways of working. They are sometimes regarded as risk takers, who operate at a tangent from others by looking at issues through a different set of lenses. Their challenge is to engage others and bring them along with them, and also translate their creativity into practical solutions.

All of these orientations are offered as an approach for leaders and team members to identify where their contributions to the team's work might be best focused. The list is not exhaustive in terms of the detailed roles. However, in our years of working with teams and leaders, these appear to be the main areas required to ensure that teams perform and can meet their goals and objectives. As we said earlier, these can be used in conjunction with other team role preference identifiers if you are lucky enough to have team members who have this knowledge.

As with both Belbin and Margerison and McCann, people can have skills and aptitudes in more than one orientation. So how can you make practical use of this idea?

Practical application

As a team leader, the following checklist will be useful to help you and your team members to identify where you (or the individual team member) believe their main contributions will be. It can also help you to identify where there may be gaps to be filled by either seeking additional help or by encouraging team members to adopt more than one role. Some team leaders (the better ones, in our view) will spend time with their team discussing, 'how best we can work together'. It is at this time that you can review with the team members as to where they believe they can contribute to their best ability, and indeed where they may wish to focus to develop new skills and approaches.

The team contribution orientation checklist

Orientation	Descriptor
Relationship	Focus will be on good quality relationships in the team. Questions will tend to be about how the issues will affect the people. Tends towards collaborative and consultative behaviour. Tries to involve and build on others ideas. Appreciates and respects others in the team.
Action	Focuses on meeting the teams' objectives. Questions will tend to be about benefits and outcomes. Tends to be assertive and self-confident. Tends towards action. Will focus on getting people energized and active.
Analytical	Focus will be on understanding what is required. Questions will be about the detail and rationale of the issue. Appears thoughtful and reasoned in discussion and debate. Focus will be on understanding the detail and data presented. May show impatience with people who don't demonstrate clarity and articulacy around the topic.
Process	Focus will be about getting the job done on time and to budget, etc.... Will ask questions about deadlines, resources and procedures. Focus will be on ensuring things are on track and people are doing what's expected of them. Once an action plan has been agreed can appear unbending. May appear overly concerned if things go off track.

Orientation	Descriptor
Expert	Will tend towards contributing in one main area where they have expertise. Questions will tend to focus around their area of expertise. May appear selfish in that their only interest is in their own expert area. May be seen as dismissing others ideas when they are not as knowledgeable about the subject. May get bogged down in detail.
Creative	Will tend to focus on imaginative and innovative ways of both working and problem solving. Questions and contributions will be about ideas and how things could work. May go off at tangents when exploring ideas and new ways of working. May appear irrational and quirky to others. May over-engineer the issue.

You can use this checklist in several different ways. Firstly, as a way of assessing your own preferred orientations when working in a team. Secondly, as a template to instigate a discussion with your team about the roles that will need to be fulfilled in order to meet the objectives. You can then allocate roles and responsibilities accordingly. And finally, if you are lucky enough to have the opportunity to select your team from people already known to you, you can use the checklist to select people with the appropriate skills, abilities and inclinations.

Key points from this chapter

- Your best performance will be when you fulfil a team role that fits your character and role preference.
- Most of us have role preferences and secondary preferences.
- Role flexibility is key for success in today's organizations.
- Taking on roles that are not your preference can be developmental and fulfilling.
- Ideally a team will have a good balance of members with a range of different preferences.

5

Types of teams

As we have already established, teams form a major part of any organization's strategy and working processes. What is different in today's working environment is that there are many different types of teams. We believe it is useful for leaders, managers and team members to understand the different types of teams and the distinctions between them. This will help leaders and team members to create effective teams and operate within these teams to the best of their ability.

Most people work in a variety of different teams – as a leader you may find that your role in some teams is to be the leader (or chairperson) and in other teams you may simply be a team member. Whether you are the leader or a team member, it is important for you to reflect about and be aware of the type of team you are contributing to, your particular role within the team and the skills, abilities and expertise you can offer.

First of all, let's look at what we believe to be the most common types of teams found in organizational life:

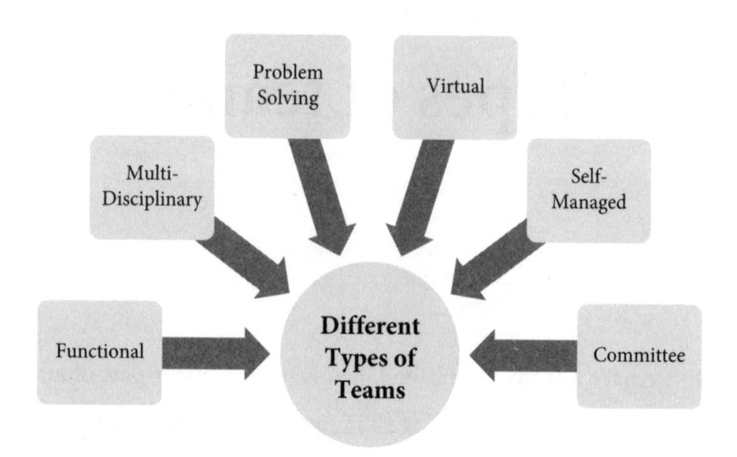

FIGURE 5.1 *Types of Teams.*

Before we progress to examine each of the distinctions and features of the different team types, let's look at some of the elements of good team working that you must consider, whatever the team type.

Any team must have an overall goal and purpose, together with clarity about the team's objectives and how performance will be measured. Every member of a team must understand and commit to this purpose and the goals, otherwise working together will be suboptimal. Involving your team in this process will pay dividends; as the team members become more engaged, the more ownership they will take for the results and outcomes. It is also worth revisiting purpose and goals on a regular basis.

We live in a complex and changing world, and teams should be aware of this and be willing to adapt and adjust to suit new challenges and situations. The following model suggests five steps for developing purpose and goals in your team/s.

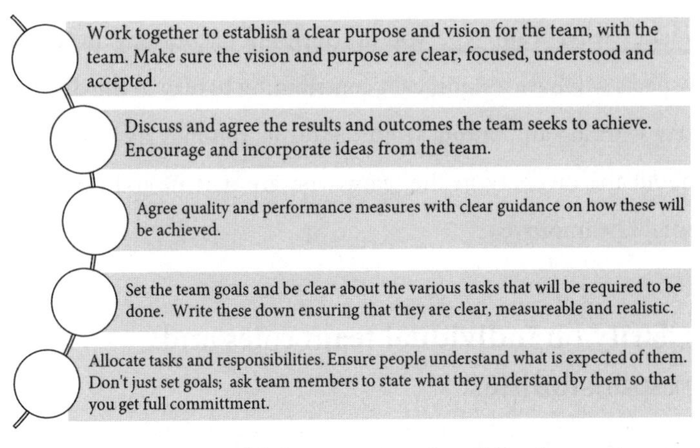

FIGURE 5.2 ***Step model for purpose and goal development.***

You might like to reflect and ask yourself about the teams you contribute to, and if you can clearly articulate the purpose, goals, performance measures as well as your role in each of the teams.

The cultural make-up of the team

Any team will be made of different types of people – personalities, nationalities, experience levels, genders, job roles, age (Amy Edmondson calls this teaming across boundaries) and all of these will contribute to the cultural make-up of the team. The key aspect of teaming across boundaries is that you can expect better ideas than if you led a completely homogeneous team. Since teams exist principally to resolve complex issues, it makes sense to have as much diversity as possible within the team. No matter what team type you are forming or working in, these aspects will have a significant contribution to play in the day-to-day working and output from the team. You may like to reflect about the diversity in the teams you are part of and how this might be improved.

Clarity on individual team roles and responsibilities

All team members must understand and be committed to their role in the team (see Chapter 4 for more on team roles). Clarity on personal goals, objectives and individual performance measures is necessary to ensure people can focus and give of their best. If you are part of a high-performing and functioning team, it will not be enough to simply understand your own role and responsibilities. It is also essential to have an overview of your teammates' roles so that you are all aware of where you fit into the overall purpose of the team. In addition to this, there must be the same degree of clarity for the overall team goals and performance.

Levels of formal and informal authority

In any team, the members will bring differing types of authority. Formal authority tends to be defined as the authority that comes with a particular role or position. For instance, the Director of Finance will typically be responsible for all things financial in their organization. Informal authority tends to be attributed to people for a range of reasons – their personal expertise, their track record, their personality, their reputation, etc.

It is an interesting exercise to identify the type of authority and the people who hold it within your various teams. This will not only highlight who has formal authority, but will help you to understand who holds informal authority and what gives them that authority.

In organizational life today, informal authority is often more important. The people regarded by others as holding informal authority are identified as 'leaders' or 'influencers' and will be those who others choose to listen to and be influenced by. These people can be hugely important in teams and knowing who they are and how they acquire that informal authority is vital for effectiveness and success in team working.

Short-term or long-term teams

Some teams come together for a very specific short-term purpose, while others are more permanent. Being aware of the proposed lifespan of the team will certainly play an important role in how the team comes together and subsequently operates. The timespan of a team will have an impact on and affect much about the team working processes. For instance, short-term teams, which we would define as teams coming together for up to a couple of months, will have to focus speedily and agree purpose, goals, roles and working processes. In this type of team, it is probably important to appoint the leader, who will tend to coordinate the teams' work and ensure that things are kept on track. In short-term teams, the members are often selected for particular reasons associated with their skills or expertise. Project, problem-solving and multidisciplinary teams are typical examples of short-term teams. So, short-term teams need to have specific elements and codes of practice and behaviour, to help them perform effectively. A good example of this type of team comes from the world of medicine.

THE HIGH-PERFORMING SURGICAL TEAM

The Royal College of Surgeons has developed a 'Guide to Best Practice' which provides a 'practical guide for surgeons and other medical specialists who work in teams and for those responsible for developing teams and improving team performance'. It draws upon the work done by the World Health Organization (WHO) on the technical process as well as the non-technical skills that every team needs, whether surgical or business – such as communication skills.

Typically, surgical teams come together to undertake a particular task and the key is to have the appropriate membership for the task at hand. In this way, you could define many surgical teams as short-term – coming together to deal with one patient operation and then disbanding. They are, of course, also multidisciplinary teams. It is possible that they never work together again with exactly the same team members, though many of the members will go on to contribute again to a similar process with another patient but with some different team members.

The key elements of the best practice guide focus on six critical attributes and in each case highlight good practice – these factors are:

- *Membership – having the right membership for the task.*
- *Leadership – clearly defined.*
- *Communication – focusing on clarity, openness, mutual respect and timeliness.*
- *Coordination of Tasks – good quality leadership and members knowing their own role.*
- *Safe Interpersonal Environment – where trust and respect are vital.*
- *Review, Reflection and Learning – to improve for future performance.*

In addition to these critical attributes (which could equally apply to any team, not just surgical teams), they also apply the WHO Surgical Safety Checklist as a way of 'ensuring coordination and communication between relevant team members thereby facilitating positive surgical outcomes'. The checklist involves the following tasks:

- *Team briefing.*
- *Sign in – a technical process to ensure correct identity and procedure.*
- *Time out – everyone introduces themselves and states their role and any concerns.*
- *Sign out – a final check that the surgical instruments have all been accounted for.*
- *Debriefing.*

The WHO introduced this checklist in 2008 to improve patient safety in operating theatres.

We can all learn from these principles and practices and adapt them to suit our own particular team situations and environments.

This case study is summarized and adapted from

The High Performing Surgical Team: A Guide to Best Practice. 2014. Royal College of Surgeons. It is available in PDF format from www.rcseng.ac.uk

While many of the same issues apply to long-term teams, there are also additional issues to consider – for instance, coping with changes in team membership, integrating new team members into an established team, keeping people motivated and committed to the team purpose and goals, and ensuring that purpose, goals, performance measures and team members' roles continue to be appropriate.

The complexity of organizational life means that many long-term teams must constantly review their purpose, goals and responsibilities in order that they remain relevant. Failure to do so can result in disengagement, low morale and a waste of organizational resources.

Features of different team types

In this section, we will highlight the key features and some examples of each of the different types of team. This will help you to reflect about the type of teams of which you may be a member.

Functional teams

These are often departmentally based and so might also be called departmental teams. A functional team tends to work towards specific ongoing projects or goals, often in service of the key strategic drivers of their organization. The people in this sort of team may have different job roles within the department, will tend to bring their own particular experience and expertise to the team and very often will have similar professional or business backgrounds. For instance, a 'sales team' or an 'HR team' would be good examples of typical functional teams. These teams tend to be permanent and long-term.

Multidisciplinary teams

Multidisciplinary teams (MDTs) are composed of members who come from diverse professional backgrounds with different areas of expertise. They bring complementary skills and experience so that they can all contribute to the work of the team to ensure effective outcomes. Multidisciplinary teams may also be known as 'cross functional'. Healthcare professions for many decades have used this type of team widely. The need of clients with complex health issues often demands a range of different skills. For instance – MDTs have been found to be particularly effective when dealing with mental health issues. When people are diagnosed with mental health issues, it is often the case that one professional cannot offer or support all of the needs of the client and their families. So a range of professionals are brought together to offer their expertise and support. In a business context, you tend to find that senior management teams fall into this category where the team is made up of, for instance, the Finance Director, the HR Director, the Marketing Director and the Operations Director. The main benefit of this sort of team is that they can all contribute from their own professional expertise and hopefully reach a better outcome because of this. This type of team can be a stable, long-term team, as in the case of a Board of Directors, or can be client-based, only coming together as a team when dealing with a single client as in the case of the mental health profession.

Problem-solving teams

These are usually short-term teams brought together to work on very specific work-based issues in real time. Typically, they will comprise of team members who have been selected for their particular range of skills and abilities and often from different levels and areas of the business. The success of this sort of team relies to a large extent on speedily engaging team members and focusing their energy and efforts onto the issues at hand. Problem-solving teams are frequently charged with developing ideas and making recommendations to a higher authority so that they can make decisions and plan implementation. This type of team offers people the opportunity to get involved with issues that are often outside their day-to-day responsibilities and can therefore be great career-development and reputation-building experiences. Problem-solving teams may also be referred to as a working party and may be a subset of another team set up to deal with a specific issue.

Virtual teams

These teams are becoming more and more common today, especially with the increase in people working from home and in global and international contexts. A virtual team is one that is geographically dispersed or remote. The team members will be totally reliant on technological communication solutions – conference calling, Skype, email, ZOOM, WEBEX, etc. So armed with a computer, access to wifi and a mobile phone, any team member can work remotely and keep in contact with their fellow team members. There are, of course, significant challenges with virtual working, not least the impersonal nature of it. The demands on the team leader to ensure good team processes are fostered and developed are much more challenging in virtual teams than in teams who meet face-to-face.

It is becoming common practice that the best virtual teams do in fact meet face-to-face on occasions, often at the outset or when there are team member changes. Meeting each other in the early days will pay dividends. Psychologically, it is easier to build rapport and trust when you make personal contact. It is also important when introducing any new members to an existing team to do this in person, as this will make integration easier. For true success, regular reviews should take place to assess and celebrate performance, progress and achievements. It is much harder to maintain good quality morale and personal motivation in virtual teams, and any team leader must take account of the need to develop ways of keeping people engaged and motivated. Many sales teams have worked virtually for many years, only coming together for sales conferences or training opportunities. However, in today's global environment, any team can work virtually and many increasingly do.

Self-managed teams

These are sometimes referred to as autonomous teams. These teams have a substantial degree of independence and control over how they work. Once they have agreed their goals and objectives with their leader (or leadership group), they work together to share tasks, implement work processes and make decisions and implementation plans. One of the main advantages of this type of team is that members are more motivated and productive due to the greater level of trust endowed upon them through the process of self-management. Having ownership of how you work is a powerful influence on performance. Research has shown that many businesspeople regard this as a key motivator. Research undertaken by Ashridge Business School, where several hundred managers and professionals were surveyed, suggested that 'autonomy – having the authority and freedom to run my own show' ranks within the top five motivators for managers. In the same report, the respondents suggest that empowering staff to take on more responsibility for themselves is a great builder of trust (The Ashridge Management Index, 2012/13).

An example of a self-managed team might be a group of peers who have come together to develop ideas and create new business opportunities. They will often be groups of people who have a common interest and are drawn together to work towards goals that will contribute significantly to their business success.

A good example of an organization using self-managed teams is Buurtzorg in the Netherlands. Buurtzorg is a neighbourhood nursing organization which has achieved outstanding results, with one consulting company estimating that if all home care in the Netherlands achieved Buurtzorg's results, there would be a saving of 2 billion euros.

The nurses in Buurtzorg work in teams of ten to twelve, with each team serving around fifty patients in a small, well-defined neighbourhood. Each team is in charge of all the tasks that were previously allocated across different departments, and there are no bosses in the team. The teams are self-governing and self-organizing.

So although self-managed teams may not be appropriate for all organizations, there is a wealth of evidence showing that they can outperform classic teams.

Committees

These are often formal groups set up by a larger group to undertake an aspect of the work on a particular topic or issue. Committees are frequently used in the public sector. For instance: 'The Committee on Climate Change (the CCC) is an independent statutory body established under the Climate Change Act 2008. The purpose is to advise the UK Government and Developed Administrations on emissions targets and report to Parliament on progress made in reducing greenhouse gas emissions and preparing for climate change' (theccc.org.uk).

Some other popular types of committees are boards of trustees and school governing bodies. Typically, committees have quite formal structures with a chairperson and members who are experts or people who are strongly interested in the issue. Some committees even have subcommittees. They usually report to a higher body and therefore tend to have formal procedures in place, such as formal agendas, regular meeting dates, rules regarding a quorum and meeting minutes. Some people may suggest that committees are groups rather than teams, as members are often elected to the committee. However, we believe that even committees can benefit from being more team-like, and leaders or chair people can learn a lot from team-working processes that will help them to run an efficient and effective committee.

Personal team type review

It is useful to reflect about the type of teams you are involved with. Most of us are involved in many different teams, both at work and outside, and all of these teams provide us with learning opportunities. It is also beneficial to think about the purpose of all the teams you are involved in so that you are clear about their contribution to the organization. So, you might find it useful to do the following Team Type Review.

- Make a list of the various teams you either lead or are involved in.
- Categorize them by team type. You may find that some teams you are in are combinations of different types: for instance, a virtual self-managed team.
- Identify the purpose of the team.
- Identify what works well in each team and why.
- Identify what doesn't work so well, what causes inefficiencies and why.
- Are there any learnings you can draw from one team that could be applied in another?
- Thinking about your own role in each team, how committed are you to the team and its purpose? What do you contribute, what could you do more of and what should you stop doing?

Key points from this chapter

- It is important to understand the different types of team you contribute to and the roles you play in each of them.

- Whatever the team type, you must take account of:
    - The overall goal and purpose
    - The team's cultural make-up
    - Who holds formal and informal authority
    - Your and others' role and responsibilities
    - The team's lifespan.

6

Qualities and characteristics for effective team leaders and members

It is almost impossible to be definitive about the qualities and characteristics for successful team leaders and members, as so much will depend upon the type of team and its context. In looking at any qualities, characteristics and skills, the main issue is to encourage good quality performance and output from the specific team, while building an atmosphere of trust, respect and harmony.

During early 2016, we conducted research with a diverse group of managers to find out their views on:

- The three skills or qualities that they believe contribute to successful team leadership.
- The three qualities that they believe contribute to being a successful team player.
- The three main barriers to team effectiveness.

Before you read the results from our research, you might like to think about how you would answer each of these questions. When you have answered them, you should assess your own level of skill or quality in the three areas that you identify in each question.

Based on the answers to these three questions, and together with our own experience of working with and in teams, we have identified a range of qualities, characteristics and skills that we believe are associated with leadership effectiveness.

Team leadership qualities, characteristics and skills

The chart below highlights the qualities, characteristics and skills that our research shows will contribute to your success and effectiveness as a team leader.

Major qualities, characteristics and skills for team leaders			
Listener Demonstrating the ability to listen to and assimilate the input and views of others.	**Shows empathy** Seeing things from team members' perspective and demonstrating understanding.	**People developer** Investing time and energy to develop team members and others.	**Fair** Demonstrates consistency by treating all team members in an objective and impartial manner.
Respectful Empowering team members by taking account of others' views and opinions.	**Decision maker** Ability to make and take decisions by using both reason and intuition.	**Knowledgeable** Demonstrating credibility and being well informed in your area of skill and ability.	**Trustworthy** Doing what you say you will do and demonstrating integrity in your dealings with others.
Compassionate Showing consideration and concern for others' welfare.	**Task oriented** An ability to focus on the tasks and goals necessary to achieve good quality team performance.	**Skilful communicator** Listening, questioning and observing with an open mind to ensure that you have good contextual awareness.	**Approachable** Ensuring that you are available and easy to talk to. Demonstrating curiosity, inquisitiveness and a genuine interest in others.
Adaptable Willing and able to flex and change to deal with changing situations and circumstances.	**Ethical** Doing the right thing based on an agreed set of principles, values and beliefs.	**Diplomatic** Treating all people in a tactful, considerate and fair manner.	**Strategic thinker** Demonstrating the ability to move beyond what is, to imagining what could be.
Supportive Encouraging and helping others to enable team members to become empowered for themselves.	**Integrity** Demonstrating honesty and strong moral principles at work.	**Humility** Showing a natural respect for others by listening and appreciating others and recognizing your own shortcomings.	**Collaborator** Demonstrating a willingness to work with others in an inclusive and productive way.

As a team leader in today's complex world, you must be able to both manage the day-to-day, as well as to cope with the unexpected and to be able to work with your team to create new and sometimes innovative solutions to the multifaceted dilemmas that arise. The qualities, characteristics and skills above will contribute to your effectiveness in both management and leadership. It is how you use these skills to engage with your team on an ongoing basis that is critical. In any team, both task and process are imperative, and if you want to create, develop and work with high-performance teams, you must focus on your own skill development. This will ensure that you are as effective as possible in taking responsibility for engaging with and developing your team.

Team leaders' self-assessment

Use the chart above to assess how well you think you use each of these qualities, characteristics or skills. Start by assessing yourself on a scale of 1 (low skill level) to 10 (high skill level). This will help you to evaluate where you could usefully invest time and energy to develop further. Select up to three areas where you believe you could further develop to be even more effective. Write down some ideas for developing in that particular area. You will also find it invaluable if you ask a range of others – team members, your boss or colleagues – for their feedback about your skill in these three areas. When you do this, try to ask for specific, detailed examples and evidence that will help you to build your skill. Use the table below to make notes.

Team leader skill – Self-development plan		
Area of focus	**What I plan to do**	**Feedback from others**
Summary notes		

Team members' qualities, characteristics and skills

We also researched the key qualities, characteristics and skills for effectiveness as a team player. The chart below highlights the main areas identified. Some of these are the same or similar to those required for successful team leadership and some are quite different.

Major qualities for team players			
Supportive Demonstrates courtesy and consideration and encourages other team members.	**Reliable** Demonstrates dependability and consistency and gets things done.	**Sharing** Knowledge, experience, ideas and generally keep other team members in the loop.	**Listening** To show understanding, consideration and engagement.
Flexibility Willingness to adapt and adjust to take account of the needs of all team members and changing circumstances.	**Open minded** Is positive and approachable and shows a willingness to take account of others' ideas and opinions.	**Appreciate difference** Demonstrates respect and tolerance of individual difference.	**Resilience** Ability to deal effectively with setbacks and to overcome difficulties and bounce back.
Self-awareness Demonstrates an understanding of the impact of own behaviour on others.	**Responsibility** Demon-strates accountability for their actions and task responsibilities.	**Participative** Contributes to the work of the team and work towards a common goal.	**Trustworthy** Has developed a credible reputation and earns trust and respect of others.
Respectful Shows interest by actively listening to other team members and values others' contributions.	**Curiosity** Demonstrates an inquisitiveness and interest to learn.	**Loyalty** Shows an allegiance to the group and fulfils commitments.	**Goal-oriented** Clearly understands and works towards the team goals.

For any team to be effective, the members of that team must demonstrate the appropriate behaviours and attitudes. This will mean that the team can work productively. A good starting point to enable this to happen is to encourage your team to assess themselves against the above sixteen key characteristics. This could perhaps be done as part of individual performance review discussions or as part of a team-building or team-development event. Encouraging your team to reflect about success characteristics for themselves is another possibility. Such discussions can be very useful in developing team cohesion and commitment, as all team members feel involved in the process.

We often use an exercise on our leadership development courses where we ask teams who will be working together during the programme to discuss and agree a charter for success, and a range of skills against which they will assess their performance. We believe that this is an essential aspect of effective team working and also encourages discussion and debate about what's necessary for good quality contribution and outputs. The teams then go on to work together on a range of tasks and are asked to review and assess their performance after each task against the criteria and to plan improvements for future tasks. You could think about how you might incorporate such discussion in your team to agree your own range of characteristics.

Main barriers to team effectiveness

Our third research question focused on barriers to success. By far, the most common answer was 'lack of communication', with lack of clarity, lack of trust, big egos and poor leadership as the next four most frequently mentioned. We highlight these issues in this chapter so that as a team leader you can be aware of the main barriers to your team's success. Awareness is paramount here, as is dealing with any issues that arise in an efficient manner. So, for instance, if you notice friction between any of your team members, it is important to deal with it quickly before it develops into something far bigger, which could then lead to low morale and poor motivation.

Main barriers to team effectiveness			
Poor communication	Lack of clarity	Lack of trust	Individual egos
Poor leadership	No common purpose	Silo working	No appreciation of diversity
Lack of vision	Lack of integration	Colleagues' behaviour	No adaptability

Team review and feedback

Because it is your responsibility as a team leader to be aware of any issues that are affecting the effectiveness and performance of the team, you need to ask your team members for feedback on a regular basis. If you invest time in building good quality relationships with the team, getting feedback will be made much easier as the members will feel comfortable sharing their thoughts and feelings with you. It is worth getting into the habit of holding regular reviews with the team, as well as with each individual member. The following questions are a sample of the type of question that will be of use to help you assess if there are any problems that you need to investigate.

- On a scale of 1 to 10 (1 being ineffective and 10 being extremely effective) how effective do you think we are as a team? Am I as a team leader? If the score is less than 10, then there is room for improvement so you must ask a supplementary question such as – What could we do to increase our score to nearer 10? Or, what small steps could we implement to move one point higher?

When reviewing team performance after a meeting or project completion, ask:

- How could we have been more effective in undertaking this task?
- What would make this team more effective?
- What have been our (or the team's) biggest challenges recently?
- What would you do differently to enable our team to be more effective?
- What specifically could I do that would help you?

Getting into the habit of doing regular team reviews and asking your team for feedback has several benefits:

- It helps build good quality relationships between you and your team members.
- It can improve morale and motivation of team members.
- It helps to build trust, respect and openness in the team.
- Your behaviour will model the behaviour for the team and its members.

Problem issues can be identified and dealt with speedily. It is, however, vital to be sure that once you engage in reviewing and seeking feedback, you must also do it both on a regular basis and in a genuine and sincere way. You must also ensure that you act on the information you receive.

> *We can't just sit back and wait for feedback to be offered, particularly when you are in a leadership role. If we want feedback to take root in the culture, we need to explicitly ask for it.*

Ed Batista, Executive Coach & Lecturer.
Stanford Graduate School of Business.

Key points from this chapter

- Team skills will contribute to effective performance and output.
- As a team leader, it is important to understand how you are performing in this role by asking others for focused feedback.
- Encouraging your team to review their performance and to build a development culture will contribute to quality performance.
- Investing time to identify the qualities, characteristics and skills important for your team is valuable for both individual and team development as well as for overall team success.

7

Building trust

A team is not a group of people who work together. A team is a group of people who trust each other.

SIMON SINEK, AUTHOR OF *START WITH WHY: HOW GREAT LEADERS INSPIRE EVERYONE TO TAKE ACTION*

Trust between team members and within any team environment is crucial to what makes the difference between a group of individuals working together in service of their objectives and a high-performing team. General Stanley McChrystal in his book *Team of Teams* writes about how the formation of the US Navy's elite SEAL teams is less about preparing people to follow precise orders, and more about developing trust and the ability to adapt. Research also shows us that there is a higher return on shareholder investment, in firms where employees trust senior management (Watson Wyatt 2002).

Other studies tell us that trust in management is the most valued determinant of job satisfaction, and that people who trust each other work more effectively together. This is something that we all feel instinctively. If there is a lack of trust, then the team will not be honest with each other, will not confide in each other and will not be able to rely on each other. You could say that trust is at the heart of the team.

But what is trust, how is it created and how do you maintain trust within teams? This chapter will define what we mean by trust and will illustrate ways of creating, building, developing, maintaining and deepening trust within team environments.

Like many aspects of leading and building teams, it takes time and effort to ensure trust is established between all team members including the leader. It does not happen overnight, it grows rather than just appearing and it requires a concerted effort where all team members must be involved in the process and committed to maintaining and deepening it. It is a two-way process, so it is reciprocal. In essence, anyone working within a team wants to know that they can count on each other, and the more effort directed towards developing a trusting environment and mutually respectful relationships, the more successful and productive a team would be. Trust is personal; in other words, we trust people, not organizations. Trust is the foundation upon which your team will be built. Without trust, the word 'team' is redundant – as Simon Sinek implied. Without trust, you are simply a group of people working together and possibly not that effectively.

What do we mean by trust?

David Maister created an equation to illustrate what he believed trust to be. This well-known but somewhat unscientific formula is where trust is a function of three things – credibility, reliability and intimacy divided by how self-oriented (selfish) you are. This is illustrated below:

$$\textbf{Trust} = \frac{\textbf{Credibility + Reliability + Intimacy}}{\textbf{Self-Orientation}}$$

This is a great starting point for understanding what trust means between individuals. Maister suggested that trust is a combination of elements which all operate together to create an environment where team members have developed high-quality connections and relationships with each other. **Credibility** is about an individual's impact. Is their behaviour consistent and do they have the knowledge, skills and expertise that they claim to have? In essence, do their actions give others a feeling of authenticity and genuineness? **Reliability** is about dependability.

Can you be counted upon to deliver your promises? **Intimacy** is about your ability to build, develop and maintain relationships with others.

Self-orientation is where individuals are solely focused on their own needs and too much self-orientation will detract from trust. In fact, self-oriented people will find it almost impossible to establish long-lasting trusting relationships with others as they are more concerned with their own well-being than with the well-being of the team as a whole.

As an example, you might have a high level of credibility with the others in your team; you are also a reliable team member and have worked hard to develop your team relations. This means that you have a fairly positive top line score. You believe your self-orientation is relatively low as you are more others focused than self-focused. Such a pattern would indicate that your level of trustworthiness in the team is high.

In addition to the above criteria, we would like to add a couple of other characteristics that we believe contribute to developing trust within a team: **Integrity,** where an individual demonstrates that they abide by a set of principles and beliefs that contributes towards their behaviour with and towards others – for instance, consistency, fairness and professionalism – and **Honesty,** where truth and sincerity are demonstrated within the team.

Trust is a difficult concept to measure and often people talk about the general feeling they have about others – sometimes referred to as their 'gut reaction'. If you apply the five characteristics explained above and recognize that self-orientation will detract from trust within any relationship, then you will be starting the process of building trust with others.

Dennis and Michelle Reina (2015) suggest another interesting notion of trust in their book *Trust & Betrayal in the Workplace*, where they suggest three types of transactional trust.

- **Competence Trust** – this is where we trust in a person's capabilities to do something. So, in a sports team, if you pass the ball to another team member, you might expect them to catch it. Or, in business, if I ask someone to deliver a seminar for me, I hope that they have the competence to deliver it successfully.
- **Contractual Trust** – where we place our trust in people's characters. We trust them to respect agreements and keep promises. This is clearly an essential part of effective teamwork; if this type of trust is broken, then a team cannot perform effectively. For instance, you might ask an experienced colleague to stand in for you at a meeting to put forward the team views on a specific issue and you trust they will actually do it, using the agreed content.

- **Communication Trust** – where we trust people not to disclose secrets, to respect confidentiality and to tell the truth. For example, you have told someone something in confidence and yet you find out from another team member that this confidence has been broken.

Clearly, we need all three types of trust within teams, and we need to be specific about the type of trust and the degree of trust. It's not that useful to say, 'I trust you', or 'I don't trust you', without having firstly discussed and narrowed down what we actually mean by trust. So, for instance, if you use the three types of trust above, you can start to narrow down the specific types of trust you are talking about. For example, you might fully trust your colleague to tell the truth and to keep her promises, but still not trust them to run your workshop! However, with some training and competence trust can be developed.

Trust is definitely one of the processes that need to be discussed up front when you are creating the team.

LESSON FROM THE MILITARY

***Dominic Mahoney**, a former Captain in the British Army, believes that the time taken in creating team bonds and trust is time well spent. Clearly, there is a difference between military and civilian teams; military teams are often formed* *in the context of crisis. Lives are at stake so there is a need to come together very quickly and work effectively. There is a strong bond between team members when there is a risk of stepping on a mine or there being an ambush around the corner.*

Civilian teams could try and echo this by creating a context where they have to work closely together for a period of time, get to know each other, build trust and create strong bonds. In the military, there is a difference between what happens in the field and what happens back in barracks. The relationships in the field are often informal, with lots of mickey-taking, even towards the leader. So a sense of humour and a lack of ego are a critical component for the good leader.

Creating and maintaining the culture of trust in a team

Building and creating a culture of trust within a team takes time and effort, and involves everyone who is part of the team. It is important to recognize that, as a team leader, you can do much to create the right environment and provide opportunities for members to develop and build trust. However, for trust to be part of the team's DNA it must be between all team members and not just the leader and each member.

So what can be done to build and create trust? Firstly, as the leader, you must model behaviour, so it is important that you demonstrate your own commitment to building and developing trust, not only with the team but in other relationships as well. It is important to remember that your team will observe you in a wide variety of situations, not just when they are working directly with you. So you must also demonstrate trust when interacting with others, both inside and outside the team.

The following chart headlines six ideas that can be implemented very easily. Of course, much will depend upon the nature and purpose of the team as to how much time you have to devote to building trust. However, elements of each of these ideas can be used no matter whether your team is coming together for a short-term project, is a virtual team or indeed a long-term project team.

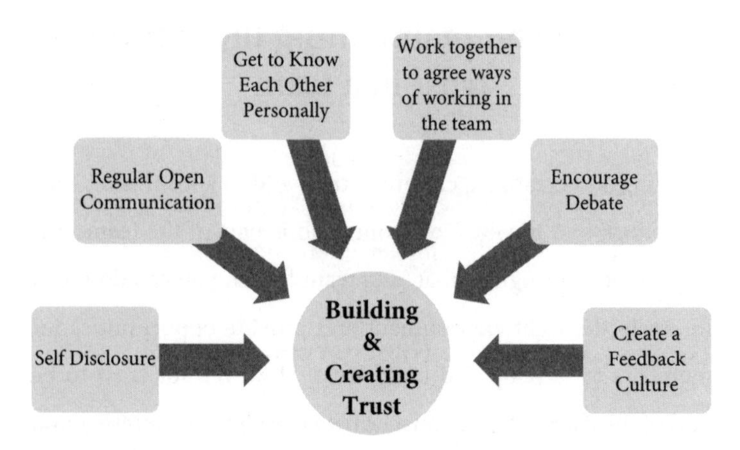

FIGURE 7.1 *Creating Trust.*

Self-disclosure

Open up to others and tell everyone a bit about the real you – not just the work-based stuff! Tell people about your hobbies and interests, the things that make you feel good and the things that upset you. The important thing here is to be genuine, and let your team get to know you.

Regular open communication

Make sure that you share information with the team in a timely and appropriate manner. One of the things that creates a barrier to trust is when the people in a team hear information 'on the grapevine' or through a third party rather than from their leader. Make sure you have regular face-to-face meetings scheduled and that you have other methods of communication established so that you can get information to people quickly and easily. Once you have shared information with the team, make sure that you create the opportunity for all team members to share and explore. They will then be able to understand what it means and any implications for the individuals and the team.

Get to know each other personally

We have found that teams that engender trust and perform well together will tend to have a far more in-depth knowledge of one another. Taking time to organize team awaydays, lunches or other events will enable you to begin this process. It can take time, as some individuals are naturally more reticent than others, but if you, the team leader, model self-disclosure, then very often team members will find it easier to follow. At meetings or other team events, encourage people to share personal data about themselves. But don't rush people; let them develop team relationships at their own pace.

Work together to agree ways of working in the team

In our experience, we find that those who spend time thinking about how they will work together and create their own rules and processes tend to be more committed and trusting of one another. In this area, much will depend upon the purpose of the team, and possibilities for discussions about how to work together are:

- Talk about the team values – what is it that each team member values about working as part of the team.
- Talk about the behaviours that team members would find acceptable or unacceptable within the team.
- Create a team charter – this is a process that we often use when running team-building development

programmes. We put people into teams and ask them to spend a little time – about 30 min – to agree the 'rules of the road' which taken together make up their team charter. This charter identifies the behaviours and rules they will follow within the team to ensure good team functioning, good quality relationships, performance and outcomes.

Encourage debate

Steve Jobs said, "Great things in business are never done by one person. They're done by a team of people." This means that teams need to be able to debate issues in an open and honest way. One measure of trust within a team is when team members feel that they can challenge, question and generally debate openly when working together. One of the main benefits of working in a team is that you have the opportunity to share and hear many different perspectives. Creating the environment for good quality debate will enable you to build trust and openness as well as to ensure better quality outcomes.

Create a feedback culture

One good method of building openness and trust is to develop an environment where feedback between all team members is welcome and common. There are many different ways of doing this. Here are some ideas:

- During meetings, whether one-to-one or in bigger groups, model behaviour by giving positive feedback in the moment when people do something that deserves it. For instance, when someone makes a good suggestion, you could say something like 'that's a great idea John, I like your focus on innovation'. Doing this, and personalizing it will not only help build trust but also confidence.
- Just before the end of a team meeting, ask each person to turn to the person on their right and say one thing they appreciated about working with them during the meeting or in the team in general. At the next meeting, use a similar process but this time ask them to give one piece of positive feedback and also one piece of developmental feedback. This sort of feedback can then be built into the regular team meeting process.
- The two preceding ideas can lead to another feedback process that can be both hugely developmental and a real trust builder between all team members. The idea is a full 360-degree feedback process between all team members. In order to get more thoughtful

and meaningful data, ask team members to write down feedback for each member of the team (including the leader). It is best to use a process here whereby individuals answer three questions – for instance:

   - What should this individual continue doing as part of their team contribution?
   - What should this individual stop doing?
   - What should this individual do to further develop their contribution to the team?

- Or the questions could be as simple as:
   - Stop?
   - Start?
   - Continue?

The purpose here is that team members share their experiences of each other as part of a developmental and trust building process.

For these ideas to be successful and for trust to be developed and maintained as part of the team's way of working, you must commit to operating and behaving with integrity. These ideas are not simply one off techniques. Each one of them must be built into the team's way of working for them to have long-lasting and meaningful results.

Key points from this chapter

- Building trust in any team takes time and effort.
- For trust to exist, all team members must be involved and committed to the process.
- Trust is largely about the behaviour of the individuals in the team and how they interact with each other.
- Adopting and practising trust-building processes will help, but in the final analysis the commitment of the team is vital.

8

Engaging the team

Culture describes the way we work around here, while engagement describes how people feel about the way things work around here.

GLOBAL HUMAN CAPITAL TRENDS. DELOITTE UNIVERSITY PRESS, 2016

Employee engagement is imperative to ensure that employees are committed to the organization, and to its mission and purpose. Good quality performance is largely due to a highly engaged workforce. As a team leader, you must be familiar with the different perspectives on how to engage a team. There are two major perspectives on what engagement actually means. One is the HR perspective, and the other is the UK's Chartered Institute of Personnel Development (CIPD) perspective. We will also share our own perspective on engagement.

The Human Resource perspective sees engagement as chiefly being composed of the following four behaviours:

- Organizational commitment – the level of desire to stay within the organization.
- The willingness to go the extra mile, and to make efforts to go beyond what is normally expected of you.
- Extra role behaviour. This is when you don't bother with defined roles but go beyond your role in order to help a client or colleague.
- Discretionary effort that promotes effective functioning of your organization. In other words, you make an effort that you don't have to, and might not even be rewarded for, but it helps the team or client.

The CIPD perspective sees engagement differently. It defines engagement as being about three things:

- Thinking about the job and how to do it better.
- Feeling positive about doing a good job.
- Actively discussing work-related improvements with colleagues.

Our perspective, gained from working with hundreds of teams and thousands of team members over a combined period of more than sixty years, is that engagement comes essentially from three things – Purpose, Involvement and Appreciation

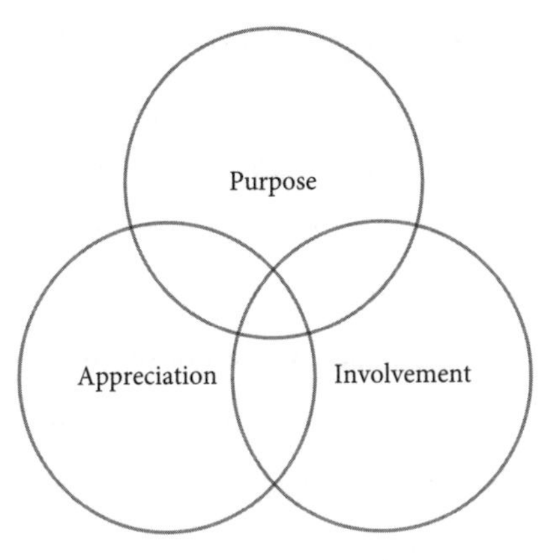

FIGURE 8.1 *Engaging the Team.*

Purpose

It is more and more accepted that for team members to be fully engaged, they need to have strong sense of purpose and meaning.

There are three levels at which you need to look for purpose – firstly, at the individual team member level, then at the team level and finally at the organizational level.

The first step is to ask your individual team members what gives them meaning and purpose in their life and how they can link that to their role. One creative way of doing this is to simply ask them what they do well. Ask them to list at least twenty things they do well at work – it's even better if you can actually sit with them and keep asking the question. Or have your team members do it in pairs with each other, then ask them to go through the list and write down how they apply this in their job and how it contributes to a sense of purpose. If they can't make the link, then simply ask them how they *could* apply it to their job.

The second level is the team level. Again the process is straightforward – you ask what the team does that contributes towards a sense of meaning and purpose in the team members' lives. Again, if you feel that the responses are not particularly positive, then you can ask what could and should the team members do – as a team – that would contribute towards a sense of purpose and meaning.

The third level is more complex in that you have less input and control over the organization's purpose. However, in order for team members to be fully engaged they do have to buy in, at least to some extent, to the organization's purpose. The challenge here, for you as a team leader, is to help your team understand the wider purpose and to make explicit links between individual team member's purpose and the wider organization purpose. You may also find that you need to influence upwards to help the organization be more explicit about its purpose.

Involvement

It is virtually impossible to be highly engaged without being involved. It's therefore essential that, as a team leader, you are careful to involve and include all the members of your team. Research by Will Schutz for the US Naval Research Lab showed that inclusion is one of the fundamental psychological needs that humans have, although we vary as to how much inclusion we need. So how do you go about involving and including your team members? Do you know how much inclusion they need or how much involvement they want?

It can be very easy as a team leader just to tell and give direction and opinions, so involving others can be as simple as asking what their thoughts are before you tell them what yours are. Stephen Covey once said that one of the habits of effective leaders was, 'Seek first to understand, then to be understood'.

We have two suggestions. The first one is for you to get into the habit of inquiring first before advocating your position. The second one is learning not to say 'Yes… but!' What we mean here is when a team member makes a suggestion and you then say, 'I agree… but', the implication is that you disagree. What we suggest you do instead is firstly look for what you might agree with in their statement, and then say, for example, 'What I like about your idea is (insert positive statement) AND we could also do (insert your idea)'. In this way, you are seeking to understand and building on your team member's idea rather than just dismissing it out of hand.

Appreciation

The need to be valued and appreciated is also a basic human need, and if you are to get successful performance from your team, then you need to be able to grasp the psychology of appreciation. We believe that team members have more energy and are more effective and creative when they enjoy their work, and one of the key mechanisms for this is to be valued and appreciated by colleagues and managers.

There are two simple steps to Appreciation, the first is *Noticing*. It's actually quite difficult to do this. You need to pay attention to what is going on around you, and then focus on what your team members are doing that is good. You need to develop appreciative eyes and ears and an appreciative instinct. You need to both look and listen for what is going well, without looking to judge, criticize or evaluate. You have to learn to ignore, at times, the things you dislike and instead focus on what is positive. You also need to try to create a culture of appreciation within the team. You need to ask yourself – Are your team members appreciative or critical in their own interactions? If your team is highly critical, then it's time to step forward and change this to a culture of being more appreciative.

The second is *Sharing*. It's not enough to just appreciate silently; you need to share it with the person or persons concerned. As a manager or leader, you might be thinking that your team gets paid for doing good work and that should be enough, but you would be wrong. What happens in this case is that you don't value and appreciate what's going well, but you very likely do notice and criticize what's not going well. So your team never hears what you do like but always hears what you don't like. This doesn't engage or energize people, quite the opposite in fact – it is demotivating. Captain Mike Abrashoff tells us in his book *It's Your Ship* that the three main reasons for people leaving the US military were:

- Not being treated with respect or dignity.
- Being prevented from making an impact.
- Not being listened to.

So if you actively want to measure how engaged your team is, then you might start by choosing one of the three perspectives above, or even better, create your own set of engagement behaviours, drawing inspiration from these three perspectives.

LESSONS FROM A JAZZ MUSICIAN

Alex Steele, a jazz musician, tells us that in a jazz band there is a need to work together collaboratively; working alone is not an option. There is a difference between jazz musicians who improvise and other musicians such as classical musicians who in essence follow the rules. Jazz improvisation is more about dialogue; it's a conversation between members of the team. This metaphor is becoming increasingly important in teams in organizations where the issues faced are becoming more and more complex, and where often there is no single easy answer – only different options and possibilities – with better or worse results.

The key skills to succeed in improvisation are deep listening, empathy, trust and an interaction of leading and following in real time. This ability of the jazz musician to step forward and lead, and then step back and follow is unique to jazz, according to Alex. In the world of work, there are lots of inequalities and hierarchies, but not so in jazz, says Alex. For him, 'jazz is steeped in uncertainty'. So members of a jazz band have to be present in the moment and aware of what's going on around them and then be able to respond. They are comfortable with ambiguity and actually enjoy it, whereas in organizations some people may not be comfortable with high levels of uncertainty. Responsiveness is a critical element in the success of the improvisation, as it would be in teams at work too.

Jazz also enjoys potential and looks not just for what is there, but what could exist, and there is an emotional element to jazz too. The musicians are empathetic and interact both with each other and with the audience. 'The tradition of jazz is one of innovation.'

Tips – in order to perform more like a jazz band to gain engagement and accountability, Alex suggests the following tips:

- *Suspend judgement – don't be too critical too quickly.*
- *Empower team members.*

- *Help team members build on each others' ideas (yes and, rather than yes, but).*
- *Create a culture of openness.*
- *Practise 'beginner's mind'. Be curious and ask good, open questions.*
- *Not knowing is okay as it leads to learning.*
- *Reframe failure as learning, because if you are not failing, you are not trying.*

We feel that when faced with engaging teams to solve so-called wicked problems that we have described earlier in the book, the jazz band analogy is a helpful one for teams. The only way to deal with these 'wicked' problems is for the team to collaborate and improvise in much the same way as a jazz band.

Why is engagement important to the team?

A number of studies have demonstrated significant benefits from high levels of engagement. Some of the findings are that high engagement leads to:

- Higher revenue growth, productivity, profitability and safety for the team and its organization.
- Better physical and mental health for team members.
- Lower absence rates in the team.

- Lower staff turnover and intention to leave organization.
- Higher organizational commitment.

These are all clearly things to aspire to in your team, but how can you be an engaging team leader?

What does the engaging team leader look like?

A summary of the research suggests that the following criteria and skills all contribute to good quality engagement.

- **Has a clear strategic vision.** The leader should also have a well-thought-out plan and ideas of how the team will work together to achieve the vision.
- **Is respected by the team.** The team leader has gained the respect and trust of the team.
- **Autonomy and empowerment.** This is about trusting and involving your team members.
- **Development.** How much do you, as a team leader, help your team develop and progress?
- **Feedback, praise and recognition.** The effective team leader is able to give positive feedback and be appreciative of team members.

- **Individual interest.** How much genuine care and concern do you as a team leader have for your team members?
- **Availability.** The effective team leader holds regular one-to-one meetings and is available for the team and individual team members. How available are you?
- **Personal manner.** The team leader demonstrates a positive approach and leads by example. What kind of manner do you have? How positive and appreciative are you?
- **Demonstrates an ethical approach.** The engaging team leader shows fairness and respects confidentiality. How fair and ethical are you as a team leader?
- **Is able to deal with poor performance.** This is a key skill because, if not managed, poor performance will affect the performance of others.
- **Reviewing and guiding.** The engaging team leader offers timely help and advice as and when necessary. How approachable are you to help, review questions and guide the team?
- **Clarifying expectations.** The team leader sets clear goals and objectives and is willing to explain them. We often see team leaders doing the first part, for instance, setting goals. But not all team leaders are so good at taking the time to explain these goals and objectives.

- **Managing time and resources.** The engaging team leader is fully aware of the team's workload, and arranges for extra resources or redistributes work as and when necessary. To what extent are you aware of your team's workload and how flexible are you at providing extra help if necessary?
- **Following processes and procedures**. The engaging team leader understands, explains, and follows relevant work processes.

Not all of these criteria will be relevant to your team. However, it's important to carry out an honest self-appraisal (perhaps with feedback from the team) as to how you measure up, and be prepared to make any necessary changes to your behaviour. Use the relevant criteria above and ask your team to rate you on a scale of 1 to 10, with 10 being excellent. Then you can initiate an open and frank conversation with your team and listen to any suggested improvements you and the team could make.

What gets in the way of engagement?

According to writer Tony Schwarz, there are five major barriers to engagement. These are:

- A lack of appreciation towards team members.
- Not showing respect to your team members.

- Treating people unfairly.
- Not listening to team members.
- Imposing unfair deadlines.

(Source: Tony Schwarz, 2010)

We also notice that engagement is affected when there has been insufficient time devoted to the storming and norming phases of team development, and when team members have not bought into the overall purpose and objectives of the team's work.

So it becomes important for you as a team leader to avoid these common traps, and to be aware of the importance of team processes and dynamics. Creating a feedback culture where you seek regular, open and honest feedback from your team should go some way to mitigating against lack of engagement.

Whose responsibility is engagement?

There is a danger when it comes to engaging the team that all the responsibility ends up with the team leader. And then there is a risk that the team members themselves abdicate responsibility. And, what happens if the team leader isn't present? Dominic Mahoney, formerly a Captain in the British Army Lifeguard Regiment (the tank regiment), an Olympic medallist and current team manager of the GB Olympic Modern Pentathlon team, tells us that too much can be made of the leader, and that the best teams have leadership 'on the field' as well. What this means is that excellent teams have more leadership in themselves than we give credit for, and this is demonstrated in sport by winning teams such as the New Zealand All Blacks (with the highest winning percentage of any team in any sport) and Sir Clive Woodward's English Rugby World Cup winning team.

The All Blacks have established what they call 'relay leaders' on the field and their process hands leadership over fully to the players for the actual match itself. Sir Clive had established different leaders on the field of play as well. This contrasts with reports in the British media about the recent Manchester United football team's process under their former manager Louis Van Gaal. He gave certain fixed instructions to the team members for different scenarios on the field. For example, when a ball was crossed into the penalty area, his players were under instructions to not hit the ball on the volley, but to take at least one touch. How can you create an engaged team when they are labouring under precise instructions that go against their instinct and good sense? The player on the field has to make the ultimate decision on what to do, not the leader, and this is the same in a high-performing team.

These lessons from sports teams can be readily applied to other teams in organizations. In essence, it means don't micromanage, make sure you have relay leaders (that is, leaders among the team who can relay the team leader's perspective) and in time be prepared to hand leadership over to the team itself.

Key points from this chapter

- Engagement comes from three areas – purpose, involvement and appreciation.
- Engagement is the responsibility of the leader *and* the team members.
- Engagement is a dynamic process that is ongoing and can ebb and flow throughout the life of the team.

9

The emotional element

Many contemporary organizations flourish when using teams effectively to organize work and make decisions. However, the true success of teamwork largely depends upon the degree of congruence, harmony and cooperation that exists within the team and between team members. Collectively, we refer to this as the emotional intelligence of the team, without which it is simply a group of people working together.

Emotional intelligence in organizational life was popularized during the 1990s with the publication of Daniel Goleman's books – *Emotional Intelligence* and *Working with Emotional Intelligence*. Goleman, together with the work of others in this area, has helped leaders and managers to better understand how feelings, behaviour and emotions can impact the effectiveness of their work.

In this exploration of the emotional element of team working, we will examine:

- What we mean by the emotional element.
- How team leaders can influence the balance between harmony and team effectiveness and output.
- How team members can contribute to their teams' emotional well-being.

The emotional element in teams

The whole concept of emotional intelligence, or EQ, has become an integral part of most leadership and people development programmes in organizational life. There are many different theorists who promote their own approach to EQ. In looking at many of these approaches and applying them to how it affects leading and working in teams, we believe that the following elements are the most important for developing success and trust in teams.

Self-awareness

Specifically being able to notice and name the emotions you experience in different situations. This self-awareness can be demonstrated and modelled to others by being able to name your emotions and having the ability and willingness to talk about these with others. For instance, if during a team meeting the conversation begins to go off track or round in circles, it can be helpful to be able to say something like, 'I am beginning to feel frustrated by this conversation as I don't believe we are progressing. Can I explain why?' By labelling your emotion you are self-disclosing a feeling without (hopefully) showing that emotion in a negative way.

You can then enter into a dialogue with your team members about why and how it makes you feel. Demonstrating and modelling this sort of emotional self-awareness will help others to understand you, and also help move the dialogue forward. It will also encourage team members to adopt this style of behaviour themselves. A less self-aware person might simply disengage from the conversation, begin to play with their iPhone, start sighing or 'tutting' or demonstrate some other behaviour that indicates frustration – none of which is productive.

Another aspect of self-awareness is accurate self-perception. This is about seeing yourself as others see you. The aim here is to reduce the gap between how you see yourself and how others see you. The obvious way to build this accurate self-perception is to constantly seek and accept feedback from others.

Self-analysis

Self-analysis is the ability to understand your own internal responses to people, events and situations. Being self-aware about your emotions is the first stage, but to be truly emotionally intelligent you must also understand the impact these emotional feelings have upon your own feelings and behaviour. So, for instance, ask yourself: When I feel angry or sad or excited, what do I do? What do I say? How do I sound? What happens to my facial expression and body language?

This involves a degree of self-reflection and observation so think about times when you have experienced difficulties when interacting with others. Think about how it made you feel, what emotions were you experiencing and how did it make you behave? Be very specific here. This type of self-analysis will also help you to understand what it is that stirs up your negative and positive emotions. This should help you to be more aware of the sorts of events, situations or people that have an effect upon your emotional responses and should assist you to think about ways of responding productively.

Self-regulation

Self-regulation is the ability to regulate your emotions and behaviours by recognizing emotional triggers and responding appropriately. Self-regulation is not about ignoring your emotions;

it is about recognizing them, being aware of the impact they have on yourself and others. Then, using them effectively, in a positive and constructive manner, to manage the dialogue, interaction and relationship for successful outcomes. This element of emotional awareness must be activated in an authentic and genuine way.

Some of the ways you can regulate and control your emotions are:

- Recognize and understand your emotional triggers, especially those that lead to inappropriate and ineffective emotional behaviour.
- Develop composure and learn to use pause and questioning as techniques to move you away from unhelpful emotional places.
- Look ahead, anticipate and rehearse ways of dealing with people, events and situations that you know might trigger unhelpful emotional responses.
- Again, if you know that certain situations, events or people are triggers, try reframing. Look at it from the other person's viewpoint so that you can respond in a more productive manner. For instance, assume that you need to get a team member to take on a new project that involves travel and working overseas. You also know that issuing instructions and telling this person what to do will meet with resistance. So a reframe might be to say something

like: 'James, we've just got this great opportunity to work with ABC Co and give you international experience; I think this it would be right up your street. How would you feel about leading this project?' So in making a subtle change in language and presentation of the issue you are less likely to experience resistance.

Others' awareness

This involves being aware of the impact of your emotional behaviour on others, and of others' behaviour on you. All of your behaviour is affected by your own emotional responses to situations, events and people – some of your behaviour is productive and some not so productive. However, behavioural responses are always situational or contextually specific, and what works in one situation or with one person may not work with another. This is the real challenge of emotional awareness. It is about being aware of the impact of your behaviour on others and of others' behaviour on you.

Our behaviour is the external manifestation of our feelings and emotions when interacting with others. It is interesting to note that some people have a natural inclination towards others' awareness, and have developed 'emotional antennae' which makes them aware of the often subtle changes in both their own and others' behaviour and the impact that this is having on themselves and others. Many people, however, are almost blind to both their own and others' behaviour. You must be aware of your own and others' behavioural changes when communicating. And you must understand the impact these changes have on the effectiveness of the interactive process. So, look out for your own and others' changes:

- Changes to body language – for instance, increased or decreased use of hand and arm gestures, or a change in body position.
- Changes to facial expression – for instance, frowning, smiling, eyebrow-raising or grimacing.
- Changes to vocal usage – for instance, increased or decreased pace and/or volume and pitch changes.
- Communication style change – for instance, inquiry to advocacy, calm to agitated, listening to interrupting, involvement to boredom or silence.
- When the general involvement in the dialogue changes – for instance, becoming argumentative, excited, critical, questioning, disengaged, defensive, enthusiastic or energetic.

Any of these can indicate changes in mood and emotional response to a situation. Being aware of how our behaviour and emotional changes affect the interaction and its progress is invaluable for building team harmony, cohesion and effectiveness.

The final aspect of emotional awareness is dealing with others. This involves skills such as influencing, coaching, dealing with conflict, engaging others, building trust and many other skills. Throughout this book we offer a range of ideas, techniques and tools for this aspect of emotional intelligence.

The team leader's role in managing the emotional element

As a leader of any team you hope that everyone in the team works together in a professional, harmonious, trusting and respectful way. However, there are always times when emotion, mood and behaviour affect the way in which the team is operating. Another thing to take into account is the sheer complexity of one-to-one relationships in a team. In a recent conversation with Swedish clinical psychologist Hans Fribergh, about relationships in teams, he reminded us that as a team leader not only do you have to be aware of, and manage, your own one-to-one relationships, but you must also have an awareness of the team members' one-to-one relationships. This means that in a team of say six people there are thirty possible one-to-one relationships. The formula for working this out is:

N (number of people in the team) multiplied by N – 1 (the number of the people in the team minus 1, i.e. you).

Take a moment to work out the number of one-to-one relationships in your own team. It might surprise you! There are of course fifteen connections but since each one must be considered as a two-way relationship, we can say there are thirty separate relationships.

The challenge for any team leader is to be aware of the general atmosphere in the team, what's going on between team members and any common trigger points for dysfunctional behaviour.

There are a number of things a team leader can do to help their team to be emotionally aware and to work together effectively. Build emotional intelligence and awareness in your team, and have a dialogue within the team about the different personality types, needs and wants of team members. You could also introduce one of the numerous personality inventories that are available as part of your team's development process, perhaps by organizing a facilitated development day for the whole team. The psychometrics we find most useful for such events are:

- Myers Briggs Type Indicator (MBTI).
- Strength Deployment Inventory (SDI).
- Belbin Team Types.

- Team Management Systems Team Inventory (TMS).
- Hogan Personality Inventory.

By using one of the above or similar, you can create a discussion about the differing emotional and behavioural needs of the various personality types. This is often an easy way of encouraging people to open up about themselves as it provides a framework to base the discussion around.

One of the important roles of any team leader is to be aware of and to deal promptly with discord, discontent, relationship breakdowns and other interpersonal issues that detract from the productive performance of the team. As we have said before, as the leader it is essential that you quickly recognize when there is any sort of friction within the team that is detracting from performance. Your main challenge is to determine what is going wrong and why. Once you understand the issues, you can begin to work with team members to get things back on track.

Good quality communication between leaders and their teams is, of course, vital for cohesion and success. As the team leader you have responsibility for establishing and guiding the communication processes. Establishing both formal and informal communication processes is vital. Some key elements of good quality team communication include:

- Setting regular team meeting dates with purpose and focus, and then making sure everyone attends.

- Ensuring all team members engage during meetings by talking and listening in equal measure. Perhaps introduce processes to be sure this happens. For instance, operating a process where people will have some time (uninterrupted is good) to state their views on topics under discussion. This type of process not only guarantees everyone's point of view is heard, but also has the benefit of developing good quality dialogue where everyone is involved. This in turn leads to better team relations.
- Encourage informal communication outside the formal meetings between teams and their leader and also between the team members themselves.
- Involve the whole team in establishing communication processes that work for them. Teams have different personalities so communication processes have to suit the particular team.

There are no set rules for communication within teams but we would suggest four key features of the process that contribute to success – **balanced contribution, good quality inquiry and listening, agreement between team members about process and involvement of all.** In fact, all team members can be involved in ensuring that these key elements take place.

You should also build and develop a feedback culture. Encouraging feedback between team members as well as from the team leader is a major way of developing emotional awareness in individuals. Some simple ways of introducing and building a feedback culture are:

- At team meetings, use one or more of the following ideas to encourage feedback. Ask each team member (and include yourself in this as well) to:
    - Say something they have appreciated about everyone's contribution to the meeting today.
    - Share with the group one thing you could be doing differently to make the team experience even better.
    - Turn to the person on your right and tell them one thing you have appreciated about their contribution to the team today.
    - Turn to the person on your left and share one thing you feel they could do more of or less of to make their contribution even better.

It is best to start the process with one exercise and build on this by using a different one each time until feedback begins to be a natural part of your team's existence.

A good example of an effective feedback culture is shown by the England Rugby Football Union's (RFU) professional referees. Under the leadership of Tony Spreadbury and his team of coaches, they have developed a strong and robust feedback culture. The referees meet with their coaches at Twickenham (the RFU's headquarters) for two days after each match to review and criticize their performance. Each referee reviews a video of their match and has to point out to their coach what they did well and where they could improve. The coach also points out areas of both effectiveness and possible improvements – so it is a two-way process. The process is extremely detailed, with both the referee and their coach having taken extensive notes before the review. The summary of this process is also shared to a larger gathering of the referee's peers and coaches with Tony Spreadbury – the head of professional referees – facilitating the process. This comprehensive and open review leads to a culture where improvement is continuous. This focus is essential as the referees come under increasing pressure and scrutiny in a game that continues to grow.

You must encourage a co-coaching culture. Peer-to-peer coaching, which is where two colleagues work together in a coaching partnership both acting as coach and coachee, is an excellent way of developing good quality relationships and emotional awareness between team members. Enable team members to draw on their own knowledge, skill and abilities to enter into co-coaching relationships with each other. You will then be building a collaborative and facilitative team environment as well as developing greater self-management and independence within the team. Peer-to-peer coaching relationships give team members the opportunity to:

- Develop a new skill that is highly transferable.
- Learn more about each other by sharing experiences and perspectives on the day-to-day issues that they are jointly working on.
- Work through real-life issues and problems and develop solutions together, which will lead to greater commitment and cohesion.
- Make best use of their knowledge, skills and abilities to help each other.

As a team leader you have a real opportunity to play a vital role in the development of both your own and others' emotional awareness, agility and acuity. This is not an easy area for many people to develop, and for most of us it is an ongoing process throughout our lives. Perhaps your most important role with regard to emotional awareness is to model behaviour for others by engaging in some or all of the ideas suggested above.

The team members' role in managing the emotional element

While a team leader has a primary role to play by creating a positive environment and introducing practices and processes to encourage and develop emotional awareness, it cannot be their responsibility alone. This is not something you do to people; team members must engage and take responsibility for their own development and emotional awareness.

Encourage team members to get to know each other. By this we mean not just knowing about each other's jobs and professional experience, but also about their life outside work. One way is to enable and encourage people to talk about their weekends or other stories related to their non-work lives. At team meetings, for instance, you could build in a little time for social chat before you get down to business. Another idea is to organize team awaydays that are a combination of purposeful fun, development and business. It is also hugely beneficial to promote discussion about emotions and feelings regarding the way the team works together on a day-to-day basis. One possibility is to get used to reviewing the process at the end of your meetings by asking:

- What went well?
- What do you think you contributed to this meeting?
- What could we do better?

By encouraging this type of in-depth reflection and discussion, you will be developing openness, trust and emotional awareness within the team.

You must actively enter into robust discussion and debate about team issues and processes, and encourage team members to reflect on both performance and outcomes. Allow them to challenge and disagree if necessary. By building an open, no-blame culture, team members will be more willing to confront and debate in an open and constructive manner.

Work together with your team to create a team charter – this is an agreement with the whole team about how you will work together – which everyone should buy into. Gaining commitment from a team with regard to the way you will work together is not something to be taken lightly. If a team is going to work actively together in an open, trusting and emotionally aware way, then buying into the charter, and the values you adopt as a team, will be advantageous.

Key points from this chapter

- Emotionally aware teams are developed through self-awareness, self-analysis, others' awareness and self-regulation.
- Emotionally intelligent teams demonstrate good quality communication skills.
- Both team leaders and members must engage in and take responsibility for their own development and emotional awareness.

10

Teams and accountability

Accountability breeds response-ability.

STEPHEN R. COVEY

The essence of teamwork is mutual accountability. In fact, we would question whether you could actually call yourself a team if accountability is absent. Accountability is about taking responsibility for your actions, behaviours and outputs. High-performing teams recognize that taking responsibility and being accountable lead to mutual trust, respect, high levels of motivation, good morale and commitment to the goals and objectives of the team. Sounds obvious, doesn't it? So how do you create the environment for, and build, an empowered team the members of which are mutually accountable?

In this chapter, we will examine what accountability means in practice, and suggest ideas that will help you to build a culture of accountability.

Defining accountability

Accountability is often seen as part of an organization's performance management process. But true accountability is so much more than that. For accountability to be truly effective it must be an integral part of the organization's culture and DNA.

Our experience of working with successful teams leads us to believe that there are three essential components that need to be present in order to create and build effective accountability. We call this the 3 C's Model.

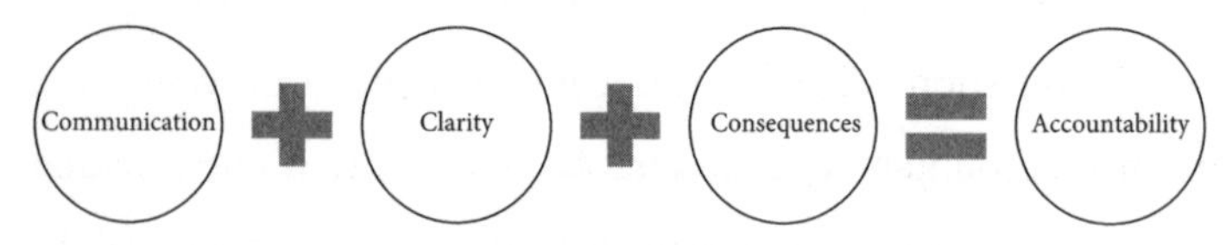

FIGURE 10.1 *Building Accountability.*

Communication

As with many aspects of leadership and teamwork, communication is a vital component. It is the glue that brings everything together. The best teams operate within organizations where mission and vision are clearly stated, explained, understood and accepted. The team must be clear how they fit into this, both as a team and as individuals. When a team understands and buys into an organizational vision, it is much easier to move to the next phase. You must identify each individual's role and responsibilities, and understand how this contributes to the overall team goal. Once team members comprehend their own role and contribution, you can then move onto encouraging team members to work together towards mutual accountability.

Clarity

One of the biggest challenges to achieving true accountability is lack of clarity. If people are unclear about or have misunderstood their direction, goals, roles or responsibilities, then it will be difficult to hold them accountable. As the team leader it falls to you to ensure that the people in your team fully understand their job role and responsibilities and how they fit into the whole. Frequently, team leaders ignore this essential element of accountability. In the rush for action and pressure for results, the conversation about goals, roles and responsibilities is often skipped or rushed. In our current complex and uncertain working environment, where teams are often working virtually, and are composed of people of differing nationalities, ages, experience levels and sometimes professions, it is even more important to ensure full understanding of responsibilities, goals and objectives. In addition to this, it is essential to also be clear about the level of individual versus team accountability. This will ensure that everyone knows whether the level of authority and responsibility rests primarily with an individual, with a few team contributors or the whole team.

Lesson from the theatre

Helena Gaunt, *Vice Principal of the Guildhall School of Music and Drama in London, spoke to us about a clarity of goals in a performance, but in organizational life we often wonder what the goal is. We agree with her and feel that it is highly important for the effective team to discuss and obtain clarity about the goals of the team. However, it can be quite rare for the team to give much time to this type of discussion.*

Helena sees this as the need to have a balance between deliberate rehearsal and unplanned spontaneity and being in the moment. No matter how much a team has planned or rehearsed, or established goals and targets, there are times when it has to respond to new situations, and here spontaneity and creativity become important.

The key thing about a performance is that you never know what's going to happen; you have to have planned and rehearsed, but at the same time you always have to expect the unexpected. There is a balance between what is planned and what emerges in the moment. There is a paradox of knowing (your craft and experience and skill) and not knowing. The same is true of the team in an organization. In a complex uncertain world, not everything can be planned, so the team must be capable of responding to new and unplanned events and adapting their goals accordingly. In these situations, they must act more like a theatre group or jazz band, and learn to improvise.

Consequences

Another of the main detractors from creating true accountability is that in many organizations and teams there are no clear consequences identified for underperformance or lack of achievement. We have observed teams which simply do not meet their targets and suffer no consequences, and this leads to complacency and overall poor performance. We also talk to people in teams who tell us that they are unaware of the consequences for non-achievement or low performance. Let's use a tennis analogy here; all the top players understand that the consequence of losing matches in a tournament can lead to moving lower in the rankings, which then affects their access to, and seeding for, the main tournaments. For true accountability to be established in any team or organization, the people involved must be aware of the consequences of non-achievement. As a team leader, you must ensure that both individuals and the team as a whole are aware of the consequences of not being accountable for goals, actions and behaviour. High-performance teams will always have a culture of clear identification of consequences. **Actions *have* consequences.** This is another area where much misunderstanding happens often because the consequences are not made clear to team members. It is also worth saying that people must be aware of the consequences of both achievement and non-achievement. This allows them to understand what will happen if they do not meet their goals and responsibilities, but also what will happen when things have been achieved. So here we are talking about both the carrot and the stick. Consequences identify to people why they are doing things and that what they are doing is important.

Accountability means that individuals, teams and organizations are clear about their responsibilities, have the authority to carry out their responsibilities, and can accept the consequences of their actions and outcomes. In fact it's all about initiative, empowerment and ownership. In teams where mutual accountability exists, there are generally good levels of trust, confidence and morale. In fact, in two recent research studies undertaken by Ashridge, the respondents identified 'having authority and freedom to run my own show' as one of the top five factors for their personal motivation.

Your role as a team leader is to work with your team and its members to create an environment where accountability exists. Taking account of and applying the principle of the 3 C's – Communication, Clarity and Consequences – is a good starting point.

LESSON FROM A PSYCHOLOGIST

In discussion with psychologist Hans Friberg, he reminds us that one of the dangers of working in a team is that certain individuals don't pull their weight. This was first discovered by a French professor of agricultural engineering, Max Ringelmann, in 1913. The experiment involved having his students pull on a rope, and he discovered that the effort exerted by a group of people pulling on the rope was less than the sum of the effort of the individuals in the group. This showed him that when in the group situation, certain individuals pulled less than they did when acting alone. This has come to be known as the 'Social Loafing theory' and it reminds us that there is a danger in a group or team of individuals not contributing to the best of their ability.

This can be counteracted by ensuring that people's performance is measured individually and that the individual's performance is held to account as well as the teams'.

Creating a culture of accountability

It is essential to take responsibility for creating a culture where accountability is a natural process for both individuals and the team as a whole. So, take account of the 3 C's as your starting point, where regular clear communication takes place alongside good quality discussions about consequences for both success and failure.

The following practical steps can be incorporated into your performance management processes to contribute towards building an effective culture of accountability.

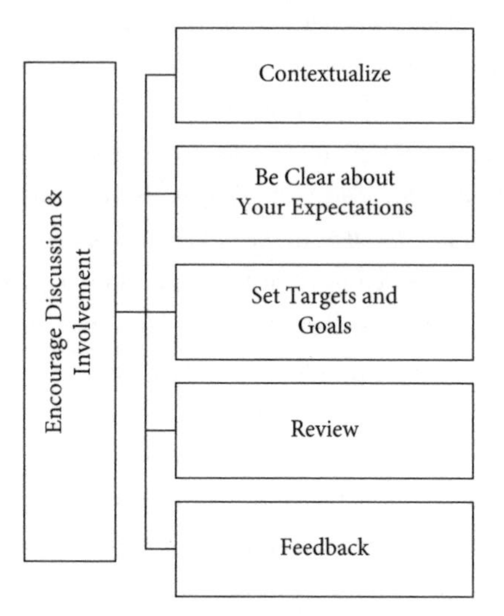

FIGURE 10.2 ***Steps for creating accountability.***

Encourage discussion and involvement

If you want to inspire commitment, then it is important to hear what the team itself has to say. Be sure to allow an opportunity for discussion about the targets and goals. Enable people to contribute their ideas and thoughts so that they feel truly empowered, and feel they have the authority to act in relation to their responsibilities.

Contextualize

By this we mean talking about the organizational vision, purpose and goals, so as to be sure that people know where they fit into the whole and that they fully understand the role of the team and the individuals within it. This should be a constant dialogue, where people are kept up to date and are encouraged to discuss and share ideas and opinions. This is all part of the process of gaining buy-in and commitment.

Be clear about your expectations

You should be clear about your expectations of both the individuals in the team and the team as a whole. At this stage, you must also be clear about the consequences for both achievement and, most importantly, non-achievement. It is at this stage that there is a lot of scope for misunderstanding, so be clear and explicit when stating your expectations. Talk about the timelines, expected results and any methodologies that should be used. Also make sure you listen to team members' expectations.

Setting targets and goals

Be very clear about individual goals, targets and objectives. Ensure that everyone fully understands their role and responsibilities, and is aware that they will be held accountable personally for achieving their individual contributions as well as for the overall team goal. Be sure to identify how you will measure progress. The more specific you are when setting targets and goals, the easier this will be.

Review

Frequent reviews of both the process and progress against targets are absolutely vital for creating a culture of accountability and building trust and mutual respect. As a team leader, you should get used to having reviews with both the individuals and the team as a whole. These reviews should be regular and not simply left to the end of a project or performance review time once a year. We live in a complex and ever-changing working environment so keeping on top of how things are going will pay dividends and will contribute to learning and team performance overall.

LESSON FROM THE MILITARY

Dominic Mahoney spent twelve years in the British Army as an officer in the Life Guards regiment, including two years as an instructor at the famous Sandhurst military academy. He saw action in Bosnia and held the rank of Captain. He is also an Olympic medallist, having won Bronze in Seoul in 1988 with Britain's Modern Pentathlon team; he remains the team manager for the British Olympic Modern Pentathlon team, which won the UK's 65th and final medal in London in 2012.

He tells us that reviewing is a vital skill. The 'after action' review is highly important in the military. After a training exercise or a real engagement with the enemy, the team will always review what happened, and this is built into all military training. The questions will be based on the following:

- *What did we set out to do?*
- *What happened?*
- *What did we learn?*
- *What will we do better next time?*

This 'after action' review is something that can be easily put in place by business teams. If the military can afford to spend time reviewing and reflecting, then surely business teams can find time to do the same. Dominic suggested that one idea would be to introduce 'bite-sized' reviews at the end of each team meeting to quickly go over the lessons learned, and to ensure better performance the next time. He also thinks that in business 'We are all wrapped up in cotton', as our mistakes don't usually have huge consequences. This can make teamwork sloppy on occasions. As in sport, feedback is critical to performance in the military. The feedback process, as to whether someone is performing, is constant and is an accepted part of the way the team works. The feedback comes immediately after the performance, not just in a yearly review.

Feedback

It is a powerful tool as part of a process to encourage accountability within a team. As the leader you should both give and receive feedback, as well as encourage peer feedback within the team. A team that is open to giving and receiving feedback is building mutual respect, trust and self-awareness, all of which will contribute to a culture of accountability. Feedback is often perceived as something negative, so you need to be ready to give positive and appreciative feedback as well as the so-called constructive type of feedback. In order to encourage and develop your own and others' skills in this area, we suggest you begin to:

- Notice what people are doing well and tell them. This is the starting point for giving appreciative feedback.
- Try to give more positive than negative feedback.
- Ask people for feedback about your performance. This goes a long way to creating a culture of feedback.
- Don't always share all the things that you don't like. People cannot assimilate too much 'constructive' feedback at any one time.

For more about feedback, you might like to refer to our book *The Leader's Guide to Coaching and Mentoring: How to Use Soft Skills to Get Hard Results.*

Key points from this chapter

- Accountability is about each individual in a team taking responsibility for their actions, behaviour and output.
- Both individual and team accountability is essential for high performance.
- Full involvement by the whole team is necessary to ensure true accountability.
- Build a culture of feedback into the team.

11

Influencing the team

Introduction

For us, influencing is an essential part of the team leadership process and indeed for any person in organizational life. We believe that to lead is in fact to influence. Recent research echoes this and confirms that leadership is about achieving influence, not securing compliance. Studies done by the Hay Group have concluded that, in the future, leaders will have to manage through influence rather than authority. As a team leader you will need to be able to influence ethically and effectively. You will find many situations in which you have to influence, whether it is influencing the team collectively, or individual team members, or other people and teams on behalf of your team.

What do we mean by influence?

It is important to be clear about what influencing is and what it is not. We are often asked if there is a difference between the words 'influencing', 'persuading' and 'convincing'. The terms are often used interchangeably, but there are some key differences. One is that persuasion always involves influencing but influence does not always involve persuasion. In other words, you can influence by other means than persuasion: for example, you can influence people unconsciously, by the way you speak or dress or by your posture.

In the table below we offer a summary of the meanings of influencing, persuading and convincing. We have also added in the word 'manipulation', which we believe to be one of the negative aspects of influence, and is another word people often ask us about.

Meanings summary

	Latin origins	**Our definitions**
Influence	Influere (to flow into)	Movement
Persuade	Per + Suadere (to urge)	To urge strongly
Convince	Con + Vincere (to conquer)	When someone moves fully towards the other person's position
Manipulate	Manipulus (handful)	To influence deviously

The diagram below illustrates our definition of influencing.

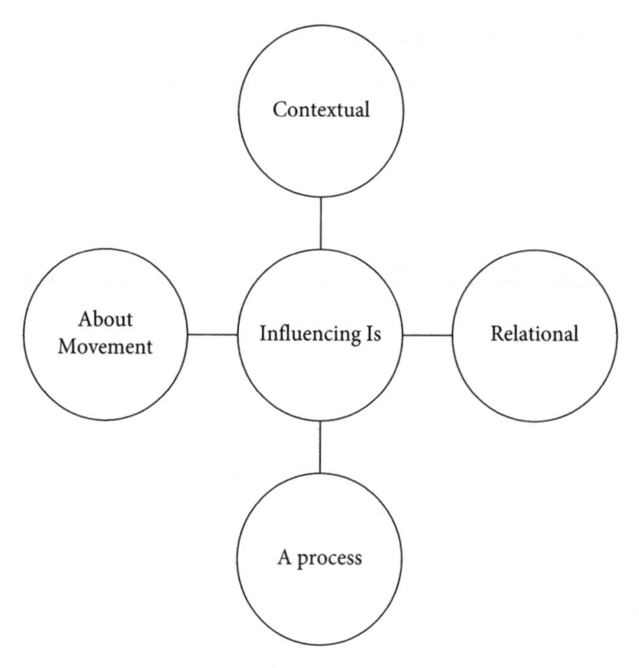

FIGURE 11.1 ***Influencing definition.***

Influencing is **situational**, in that how you influence depends on the context in which you are influencing. It is **relational** in the sense that you are always influencing other people, and therefore need to have good emotional and relational intelligence. It is also **a process** rather than a one-off event. This implies that you are likely to be influencing over a period of time and therefore you can sometimes afford to influence in small steps rather than try to immediately convince. Finally, for us, influencing is about **movement**. That means if you get some movement in the other person's position, then you have successfully influenced someone.

How do people like to be influenced?

It is thought-provoking to look into how people actually like to be influenced. Over several years, we have conducted research with hundreds of managers as to how they liked to be influenced and also what acted as influencing turn-offs. The results were interesting and the main categories are as follows:

- **Involvement:** The managers said that to be influenced effectively they needed to be involved. They wanted to be listened to, and their opinions and perspectives to be taken into account.
- **Confidence:** There was a desire for the influencer to demonstrate confidence and positivity as well as energy and conviction about the issue.
- **Appreciation:** People want to be appreciated for their contributions. This can be done by developing rapport and building a relationship that is mutually

beneficial and based on likeability. Having a positive relationship with others means they are more likely to listen to you.

- **Credibility:** Managers told us that influencers need to establish a certain credibility. This can be achieved by having a good reputation and of course sound knowledge and a good track record.
- **Evidence:** There was a strong need for sound arguments, logic and data to support the influencing case. Where possible, the influencer should bring in any relevant research to back up their argument.
- **Clarity:** Managers told us that they liked clarity and wanted influencers to be articulate but concise. They hated 'waffle' and beating about the bush.
- **Passion:** The expectation is that as an influencer you will demonstrate a level of passion and energy about the idea, which in turn will indicate self-belief and confidence.

In terms of what turned them off and made influencers ineffective, the managers identified five main reasons.

- **Being patronized:** Managers felt that influencers who were condescending towards them were a real turn-off.
- **Being put under pressure:** It was felt that being put under pressure to do something or using 'hard sell' tactics was counterproductive.
- **Using authority:** The exclusive use of formal or position power was viewed as somewhat ineffective. It was felt that if someone could not convince them with good reasons and had to resort to their formal authority, then they had failed. They might have to comply but would not be convinced.
- **Asking for, then discounting, ideas:** This was a major turn-off. It happens when people *appear* to ask for your thoughts but then go on to completely disregard them.
- **Feeling manipulated:** This is when managers felt that they are being deceived and misled. They might initially have been influenced but when they realize they had been misled, any influence is destroyed.

These ideas were expressed by a broad range of managers and leaders who work at all levels in organizational life and in many different roles and professions. In summary, it seems to us that, when being influenced, people want three key things – *involvement*, *clarity* and *authenticity*.

The use of formal and informal authority

To get things done in the team, the team leader has two options. One is to use their formal authority; the other is to use a more informal authority, which we describe as influencing without authority. People will not do what you want if they don't know what you want – so there is a clear basis for at least communicating your goals. You can do this in two ways. One is to tell or order people to do what you want. This may work for some people in some organizations, some of the time, but generally it's no longer an effective way of getting things done. And even if you do use this approach, there are skilled and unskilled ways of doing it (more on this later).

So how do you get things done if you don't tell people? You need to get their commitment to doing something they perhaps were not originally going to do – in other words, you are going to try to influence them to see things from your perspective. This is when you are influencing without authority.

A further argument in favour of using an influencing style, rather than a command or tell one, is that it builds sustainable team leadership. When you order someone to do something, you are building in the necessity to keep on giving orders; if you rely too much on formal power, you run the risk of ending up with employee compliance rather than employee commitment.

Use of formal power in a team environment is neither effective nor efficient. Control leads in the end to dependency, but by using an influencing approach you devolve power to the influencee. This of course implies that the influencer must be open to being influenced. If you only ever want to be the influencer, then you are commanding and telling, but under a different name! In effect, a large part of the team leader's job is to discuss things with peers and bosses, and is not just about the simple delivery of orders to team members. In this type of situation, negotiating or influencing skills become paramount, because the option of using formal power is no longer available.

Four approaches to influencing

Research shows us that people use four main approaches to influencing others: Assertive, Participative, Logical and finally, Inspirational. Ideally, the team leader will be able to skilfully use all of these approaches depending on the needs of the situation. In practice, we find that most people have a preference for one or perhaps two of these approaches, and often find one of the approaches difficult to use. A typical manager might have a preference for logical and participative approaches, and have inspirational influencing as their least preferred approach.

In the chart below, we have summarized some of the key words associated with each approach.

Assertive	Participative	Logical	Inspirational
Telling	Involve	Facts	Vision
Power	Listen	Analysis	Narrative
Pressure	Appreciative	Detail	Metaphors
Confidence	Inquire	Proof	Symbols
Fast paced	Build on others	Reason	Energy
Persistent	'Yes, and'	Evidence	Images
Authoritative	Charm	Lack of emotion	Future

Brent and Beech (2011).

It is important, therefore, for you to understand your own preferred influencing approach and to be aware of your team members' preferences as well. You will then be able to choose the most effective influencing approach for your team members. One simple way of getting an initial idea of your preferred style would be to use the table above and select the word from each row that best describes your influencing approach – the style with the most selected words might then be your preference. By identifying your strongest preference you will also identify the areas where you can further develop your influencing style for greater flexibility and effectiveness.

Tools and techniques

There are a huge number of influencing tools and techniques that the team leader can use, and we have written extensively about these in our book *The Leader's Guide to Influence*. In this chapter, we will focus on a few very effective tools. The diagram below indicates those we will discuss:

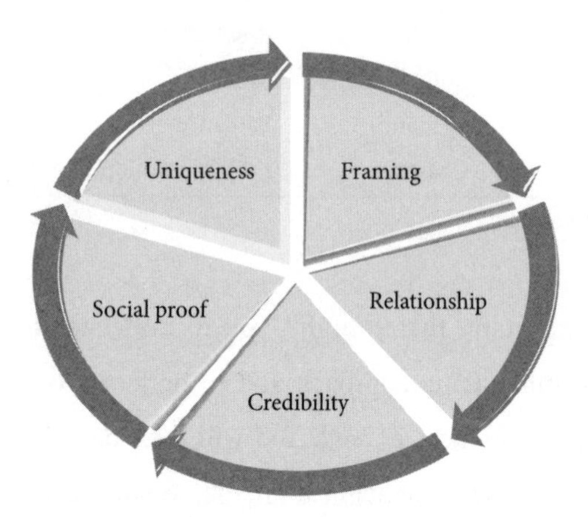

FIGURE 11.2 *Effective influencing tools.*

Framing

As we mentioned earlier, frames are the mental structures that allow us to understand reality – and sometimes to create what we take to be reality. For Harvard professor Amy Edmundson, a frame is a set of assumptions or beliefs about a situation. For us, it's about how we manage the meaning of an interaction with someone, focusing on the perspective you want to share with the others. So it is clearly important to understand how you are framing a situation, and how your team members are framing it. You will also need to know how to reframe effectively in order to influence.

For instance: let's say someone in your team is underperforming and you start to think of them as a 'problem performer'. You are in effect framing them as a problem and the danger is that if you continue to frame them as a problem, then that will affect how you behave towards them. The concern is that your behaviour towards them simply reinforces the situation, because you are more likely to be short-tempered with them, and ignore any positive aspects of their behaviour. What you can try to do is to reframe the situation by looking at when the person has *not* been a poor performer, and by looking at something that this team member does well. You are then more likely to be appreciative of these things, and start asking questions about the perceived poor performance in a calm, nonjudgemental way. Reframing your perspective in this way enables the team member to refocus their energy and efforts in a constructive way.

There are many ways of reframing. The simplest and most obvious example of reframing is the 'glass half-full, glass half-empty' analogy. Framing the glass as half-empty focuses on what you don't have; framing it as half-full focuses on what has been achieved.

When you reframe a situation, you are trying to look at it from a different and more useful perspective. For example, in an influencing situation, we usually frame the situation from our own perspective. It might be more influential to try framing it from the influencee's perspective. This is what we call the **SWIIFT** perspective – 'So what's in it for them?'

You can help your team to learn and develop by using this framing technique with them, and it can be used to influence yourself as well as others. If they fail at something, they might become despondent and de-energized, because failure is usually framed as a bad thing and is to be avoided. But you could help them reframe their failure as learning by asking effective questions such as, 'What did you learn from the failure? What were your assumptions about the situation? What can you do differently in future?'

The American inventor Thomas Edison was famously quoted as saying, 'Every wrong attempt is another step forward. I have not failed 10,000 times; I have successfully found 10,000 ways that will not work'. This attitude helped him to invent, among other things, the phonograph, the first commercially viable electric light bulb and the motion picture camera.

Relationship

It is about empathy, liking and trust. If you have no formal authority over someone and they don't like or trust you, then you will have great difficulty in influencing them. However, if you have a positive relationship and a high degree of trust, then it's far more likely that you will be able to influence them. This of course implies that you think strategically about your relationships, both inside and outside the team. You can map out the team members and then rate the quality of your relationship with each person on a scale of 1 to 10, with 10 being excellent. That is not to say that you need to have a perfect 10 relationship, but if it's less than a 5, then you probably need to focus some effort on building or rebuilding the relationship with that team member.

Some of the things you can do to improve the relationship is to be empathetic and appreciative towards other people and focus more on what they do well rather than feeling the need to be critical. Research tells us that it's more effective in terms of performance to listen more than you tell, to be more focused on your team than yourself and to share more positive and appreciative feedback than criticisms.

Relationships are also linked to emotions, and it is important to remember that being right about something does not necessarily mean you have influenced the team. You can think that you are right but remember that this not sufficient to actually influence anyone.

Social proof

We are the third most social species on the planet – after ants and bees – and so we are hugely influenced by what other people think and do, especially people who are similar to us or whom we admire and respect. It therefore makes sense when you are influencing others to try to identify the most popular or respected people in the team, and start by influencing them. If you get them on board first, then it will be much easier to influence the others.

An example of social proof in influencing is when you see buskers or street performers passing round a hat for donations. They will always either seed the hat (i.e. put some money in it first) and/or ensure that a colleague or friendly member of the audience steps up and puts in some money (preferably paper money, not coins).

When influencing your team, make sure you use examples that are relevant to the team. You might want to adopt a particular team process – so if the team likes sport, you might use the New Zealand All Blacks rugby team as an example of a successful team which already uses this process successfully. Be careful, however, to make sure that your example of social proof does actually resonate with the team.

Credibility

If you are not seen as someone who is credible by the team, then it will be extremely difficult to influence without recourse to formal authority. It therefore becomes important to think about your credibility and your reputation or how the team sees you. If you are seen as having lots of expertise and credibility in an area, then it becomes much easier to influence effectively. The question then is how do you enhance your credibility and authority with the team? This will depend on the make-up of the team and what they consider as credible. For some fast-paced sales teams, your credibility will depend on your sales ability; for other teams, it might rest on your experience and expertise, or your empathy and relational skills. So how would you describe your reputation? Where does your credibility come from? It is also critical to give some thought to your image and reputation and ensure that it is positive.

Uniqueness

What distinguishes one product or service, or indeed one person from another, is how distinctive or unique they are. Although we realize that every human being is unique, it is a fact that some stand out from the crowd more than others.

The big danger for products or services is that they might be seen as a commodity, and therefore be considered less valuable. So how does an organization differentiate itself? If, for example, you have ten Estate Agencies on your High Street, how do you choose which one to use? The answer is differentiation. Which one is the friendliest? Which one is the most efficient? Which one has the best customer service? Which one can you trust?

Although we as humans can never be seen as commodities, there is a danger that when influencing we are not seen as being unique enough, and are therefore less effective as influencers. So the question becomes, what makes you different? What is your USP (unique selling point)?

One way of being more unique is to tell a story. Humans are natural storytellers and stories resonate with us in a much more compelling way than pure logic, so try to create a story and a narrative rather than just giving the facts. Professor Mark Turner, in his book *The Literary Mind* (1996), says that most of our experience, our knowledge and our thinking is organized as stories.

The essential difference between reason and emotion, according to Canadian neurologist Donald Calne, is that reason leads to conclusions, while emotion leads to action. So don't forget to bring in the emotional element to your influencing; telling a story is an effective way to achieve this.

Finally, influencing is a two-way process in teamwork. As a team leader you need to be able to influence the team but also be open to being influenced by it. To influence effectively means using tools, principles and techniques such as we have described above, in a skilful, appropriate and ethical way.

Key points from this chapter

- Influencing is a critical skill for team leaders.
- It is important to understand your preferred influencing approaches.
- Be willing to flex and adapt your approach to suit the situation and people you are influencing.
- Think about how you are framing your position and reframe if necessary.
- Influencing is situational, is relational, is a process and involves movement.
- To be influenced, people look for involvement, clarity and authenticity.
- Influencing is a two-way process in teamwork.

12

Facilitating the team

What do we mean by facilitation?

To facilitate the team is to be a change agent and help the team to develop and improve performance. Any team member acting as a facilitator will also help the individuals in the team to develop and improve their performance, and they will be focusing on how the individuals contribute to the team. The term first came to prominence with the development of quality circles in the 1970s. It was found that these teams of people needed someone to facilitate the process of coming up with improvements. The facilitator wasn't there to solve the problems, but to help the members of the quality circle to have the means and processes to solve the issues themselves. The word 'facilitator' comes from the Latin word *facilis,* which means *easy*, so the facilitator is literally there to make things easier for the team to work together.

Why facilitate?

What often happens in teams is that there is a clear focus towards action and finding the answers to the problems. Unfortunately just being focused on solving problems doesn't necessarily make the team any better at actually solving these issues. So a good facilitator looks at three key areas of teamwork: The WHAT, The HOW and the WHO.

- The **WHAT** is the work the team is engaged in – in other words, the task.
- The **HOW** is the process of accomplishing that task.
- The **WHO** consists of the relationships and dynamics between the team members.

The HOW and the WHO are more important than the WHAT, because they are instrumental in defining how the task gets done and if it is done effectively.

Facilitating the HOW – the process

Teams often focus on the people but overlook the *process* of how the team is working, and that is a mistake, because the problems faced by teams are mostly linked to the process of how they work together. The facilitator will specifically look at these processes and make the team aware of HOW they work together. So what are these processes? One good example is listening. Do the team members actually listen to each other, or are they constantly interrupting each other? Clearly, a team that doesn't listen to each other cannot be very effective. Another example might be inclusion. Who is included in the conversations? Is one person dominating? Does everyone get a fair chance to speak up? Are some members being denied the opportunity to speak? Are some too shy to contribute? And what about trust (see Chapter 7)? Do the team members trust each other? Clearly, if there is a lack of trust in the team, it will not be as effective as it could be. Who has the most influence? Where do they get the influence? Is it because they are the most experienced person, or simply the most powerful, or just the person who shouts the loudest? Just because they have influence doesn't mean they are right.

We frequently run experiential exercises for teams during our training sessions at Ashridge. We have noticed that what often happens is that, when faced with a problem to solve, a couple of extraverted members come up with some ideas and are not shy about expressing them. These then get implemented but often don't actually work. What no one has bothered to do is ask the quieter, more introverted members of the group, who haven't yet said a word, what they actually think. Very often, it's their ideas that turn out to be the good ones.

Will the team address these issues if left to its own devices? Our view is that it will not. In our experience, teams like to focus on getting things done and do not have the experience or capability to address the kind of issues we are talking about here. This is where facilitation can play an important role.

One example is a team Mike worked with in Sweden. The team was set up as a project group to come up with solutions to some of the strategic issues faced by the firm. Although all the members were managers and quite experienced, they did not appear to have much knowledge about the basics of teamwork, and worked rather slowly together. There was a lack of creative and strategic thinking.

They were all very hardworking, extremely cooperative and showed a high degree of willingness, but did not appear to be able to stand back to reflect and view the project from different angles. They did not have much practice in building on each other's ideas or managing the team process. They were very action-oriented, extremely practical and pragmatic, but not so strong on conceptual, strategic or creative thinking. They were also very strong on technical issues, but had rather a lot to learn about group and team dynamics, communication and people management in general.

We could describe many of the teams we work with in this way, that is, technically strong, pleasant, cooperative, willing, practically minded, hardworking and oriented towards results. But these undoubted qualities are not sufficient to make an effective team. These managers need to be able to facilitate the team to work more effectively together. In our experience, the ideal situation is for all team members to be trained in the art of facilitation and for different team members to take on the role at different times. This may well require some formal training beforehand. At such times, it might be a good idea to have an external facilitator to facilitate a couple of meetings to model good facilitation processes or to shadow team members for a while until they become skilled and confident.

What skills does a facilitator need?

A skilful facilitator will use a wide range of skills. The following are a range of the key skills an effective facilitator will demonstrate.

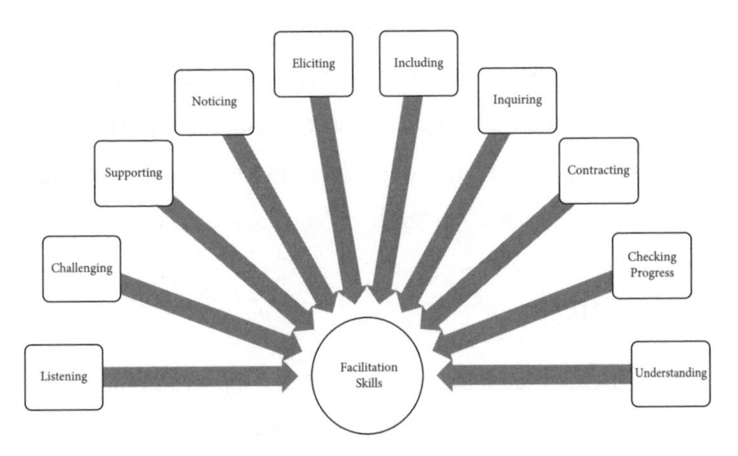

FIGURE 12.1 *Key Facilitation Skills.*

Let's look at each skill in a little more detail.

Listening

It's vital for the facilitator to be an effective listener, who can listen at several levels. Listening at different levels means listening to the obvious things such as the facts, data, language and logic, but also being able to listen more closely to the feelings, emotions and assumptions that are implied. This means also listening for what is *not* said.

Challenging

There are times when the facilitator will need to be able to challenge team members, and there is a real skill to challenging effectively. Striking the right balance between challenging and supporting is difficult. Challenge has to be made in a skilful way. A good challenge will be one that does not attack or blame the person, but rather focuses on the issue at hand. A poor challenge is likely to upset the person and uses emotive and non-specific language, such as 'that's rubbish' or 'you are always doing that'.

Supporting

Clearly, the team facilitator's main role is to support and encourage the team to work well together. So encouraging, appreciating and supporting the team as a whole, as well as individual team members, is an important skill. We think that having a balance of around three or four to one between appreciative remarks and critical remarks works well.

Noticing

What we mean here is that the facilitator has to observe and notice what is going on in the team. What is the atmosphere like? What are the undercurrents? What are the emotions in the team? One way of picking up on emotions is to be aware of the non-verbal communication in the team. What is the body language? What kind of tone and language are team members using with each other? Albert Meharabian estimated that when the subject was an emotional one, up to 93 per cent of any communication could be nonverbal.

Eliciting

By this we mean the ability to create trust and bring out what a person really thinks. This means encouraging people to come forward and to speak up openly and honestly.

Including

Inclusion is one of the fundamental human needs, and any facilitator needs to be careful to make sure that everyone has a voice in the team. It's very easy for certain team members to dominate a conversation. They may be highly extrovert or more confident than others, or they may simply like the sound of their own voice. The facilitator must intervene and make sure that everyone has an opportunity to talk and is able to speak up, and that no one person or group dominates the conversation. Another thing he/she needs to look out for are people interrupting each other. There is really no excuse for people interrupting someone else. If a person is being too long-winded, then you as facilitator can gently and diplomatically intervene and ask them to clarify and/or summarize their point.

Inquiring

The skill of inquiry is similar to that of eliciting information, but is all about asking good and open questions together with effective listening. The skill here is to be able to ask and probe, without making judgements about the responses. This can be more difficult than it sounds, as we often observe team facilitators asking too many closed questions, or not probing deeply enough into an issue, or worse still, making critical remarks.

Contracting

it's important for the facilitator to contract with the team so that everyone is clear about the purpose and process of the team meeting. This covers the essentials like timing, but also issues such as confidentiality and what kinds of behaviours are desirable, and those that are not acceptable to the team. For example, the facilitator might ask the team what the protocol should be around using mobile devices in team meetings.

Testing understanding

It's essential that the facilitator is able to check people's understanding during the meeting. As such, they need to constantly listen, observe and notice when there seems to be any confusion or a lack of understanding between team members. One way of doing this is to intervene and then paraphrase, by saying something like, 'If I understand you correctly John you are saying …?' So you are essentially rephrasing what John has said but in a way that is hopefully clearer to those who haven't grasped John's point. This then allows John to agree or to further clarify his meaning.

Checking progress

One of the key roles of the facilitator is to check the team's progress. So they might pause the proceedings by asking for a 'time out' (often by making the T sign with their hands as a signal). They would then go round the team asking each person to what extent progress was being made on the issue under discussion, and also by asking what else or what more could be done. It's not uncommon for team meetings to lose focus and go off track, so it's the facilitator's job to notice this and help get the team back on track.

What attitudes?

We also believe that effective facilitation requires a certain manner and there are a number of attitudes that an effective facilitator will display. We suggest the following:

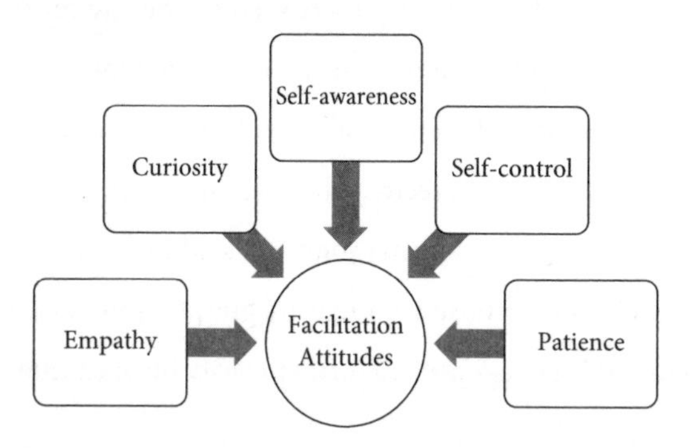

FIGURE 12.2 *Key Attitudes for Facilitator.*

Again let's look at these in more detail.

Empathy

It is critical to be empathetic but not to patronize team members. The literal meaning of empathy is affection. In business, however, it tends to be defined as the capacity to enter into and understand other's feelings and emotions. As a facilitator you must try to understand, respect and work with your team members' feelings. Remember, you are acting as the facilitator to enable the team to perform well, not as the dictator.

Curiosity

A high degree of curiosity is essential to allow you to probe and inquire and it also demonstrates interest. This must be authentic, and you need to show genuine interest in both the people and the issue.

Self-awareness

If you have low self-awareness and have no idea of how you are coming across and how team members are perceiving you, then you are not going to be an effective facilitator. So it is important that you seek, and are receptive to, any feedback that will help build and develop self-awareness.

Self-control

This can also be described as emotional management. Emotions often surface in team discussions – especially where there are areas of disagreements. The team members themselves may become angry or annoyed and express that emotion, but your job as the facilitator is to keep your own emotions in check so that you can defuse the situation for others.

Patience

Let's be honest here: facilitating the team isn't easy, and you will on occasion require the patience of a saint to do it well. If you are not a naturally patient person, then that is an attitude you will have to work on, as many of the issues you are trying to resolve will be caused by impatient team members.

In essence, the role of the facilitator is to manage, guide and control the group process, to ensure everyone is involved and that the desired outcome is met. This involves:

- reminding people of goals and objectives.
- ensuring balanced participation levels.
- bringing people in who want to speak.
- controlling people who take up too much air time.
- summarizing throughout and at the end what's been agreed.
- clarifying any misunderstandings.
- dealing with any inappropriate behaviour and remarks.
- managing time.
- concluding.
- if time allows, managing a brief process review.

A final word about facilitation. You may want to receive some training on how to be an effective facilitator, but you can also learn on the job as long as you are prepared to ask for and accept feedback on your performance. It is our strong belief that you as a team leader should learn the skills of facilitation, and if you are already a good facilitator, be prepared to develop your team members in these skills so that everyone in the team can act as a facilitator as and when necessary.

Key points from this chapter

- Facilitators literally make it easy for the team.
- All team members can benefit from being skilled facilitators.
- Attitude is as important as skill in this area.

13

Coaching the team

Introduction

Coaching is fast becoming one of the key skills for managers and leaders. The UK's Corporate Executive Board (2009) stated that coaching by an executive's manager was the strongest factor in preparing them to move into leadership positions. The Chartered Institute of Personnel and Development in the UK tells us that coaching by line managers is one of the most effective learning and talent development practices. Interestingly, their survey also suggests that it is one of the key leadership skills that organizations lack! (CIPD 2013). And, in addition to this, coaching is heavily favoured as a management style by Generation Y (Ashridge 2013).

So, it is quite clear that a team leader will benefit enormously by being able to coach effectively. The dilemma, as the quote by Myles Downey suggests, is that coaching the team presents complications that are not present when coaching individuals. Teams have different dynamics to individuals, and so we must be able to coach the team as a whole entity, but without forgetting to address the needs of the individual members of that team.

The basics of coaching

Before thinking specifically about coaching the team, you need to be able to acquire the basic skills and processes of coaching. In our book *The Leader's Guide to Coaching and Mentoring*, we offer a comprehensive guide to much of what a leader and manager

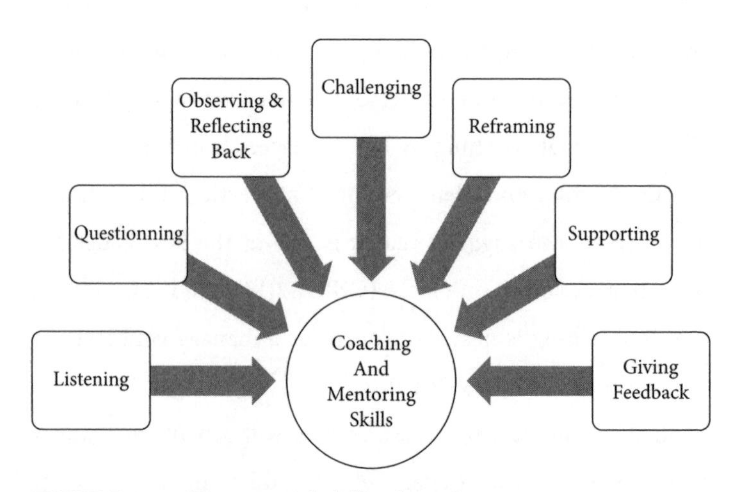

FIGURE 13.1 ***The essential skills of coaching.***

needs to know. Here we will offer a summary of some of the key coaching skills and processes.

In the diagram above we have listed the essential skills of coaching, whether it be for the individual or the team; below is a brief summary of each of these skills.

Listening

There are two key aspects at play here. The team coach must listen, not only to hear and show that they have heard, but also to listen to understand and show that they have understood. If you do not listen carefully and attentively to what a team member is saying, and also fail to listen to what is *not* said, then not only do you risk missing out on an important contribution but you will negatively impact your relationship with that team member.

Questioning

The team coach must be able to ask appropriate and incisive open and probing questions. The purpose of the question is to encourage team members to open up and offer their opinions and suggestions and also to share their genuine views and feelings. The intent of the coach is to fully understand the team members' perspectives. They should use a full range of questioning techniques to suit the coaching situation.

Observing and reflecting back

It is important to notice what is going on with the team member's body language and paralinguistics or vocal usage. Research tells us that a great deal of the meaning of any communication comes through non-verbal communication – body language and paralinguistics – and so it is important to listen beyond the words that are said and use your eyes as well as ears to notice what is really going on. Pay attention to the coherence between what is said and *how* it is said, and be prepared to challenge any discrepancies.

Reframing

According to Amy C. Edmondson, Professor of Leadership and Management at Harvard Business School, a frame is a set of assumptions or beliefs about a situation. As a team coach, you need to know what your team's assumptions are about a particular situation; then you can either support or challenge that thinking appropriately.

Challenging

It is essential to be able to challenge your team's thinking, and it's also important for your team to be able to challenge your thinking. We live in a world where many of the problems the team has to face are so-called wicked problems. These are problems that have no right or wrong answer – only better or worse options. In these circumstances, it is highly unlikely that you as team leader will have the best option for action without consulting the individual and collective intelligence of the team.

Supporting

It is important for the team coach to be able to offer support and encouragement to team members. Not all of the team will be confident to speak up freely, and if you want to encourage freedom of thought and expression without fear of judgement (which, of course, you should) then you must be supportive of team member's participation, even if their ideas are not always brilliant.

Giving feedback

Giving feedback to team members will be an important part of any team coach's role. What we can confidently say here is that team members will want and expect feedback from you, and you should be skilled and confident at giving it in an appropriate way. As previously stated, striking the right balance between appreciative and constructive feedback is the key to success.

Coaching models and processes

There are many different models and processes the team coach can use in order to have a structured approach. Here we offer a summary of three models:

- Sir John Whitmore's **GROW** model, which we have adapted slightly.

- The Appreciative Method of coaching.
- Solution Focused coaching.

The GROW model

The team coach can use this model to find out the team's Goals, Realities, Options and Will. The idea is that the coach explores the coachee's specific goals and objectives, and then moves on to exploring what is going on in reality, what has been happening, what people have done and said, who is involved and so on. The coach then asks the coachees to develop a number of different options, before moving on to asking about the degree of will or commitment, and what energy the coachees have in order to take specific actions. GROW can appear to be a fairly obvious model, but it helps you to take a more structured coaching approach rather than just giving advice, so in practice it is very useful to have a model like this. In reality many managers start to coach without having fully explored the specific goals and then find themselves stuck.

We have created a modified version of this structure and added a couple more R's to the process (GRRROW). The first extra **R** reminds us to specifically ask about relationships, as well as for facts and figures.

- What are the feelings in the team?
- What is the emotional reality?
- Who else is involved and how are they feeling?

There is a real danger that managers will be tempted to skip the emotional realities involved!

The other **R** we add is for Resources, by which we mean what are the strengths and resources that will help the coachee/s to move forward. When have they been successful in addressing similar issues, for example? What are the resources and competences that will help them resolve the issue? You cannot focus simply on what the coachee or team is unable to do!

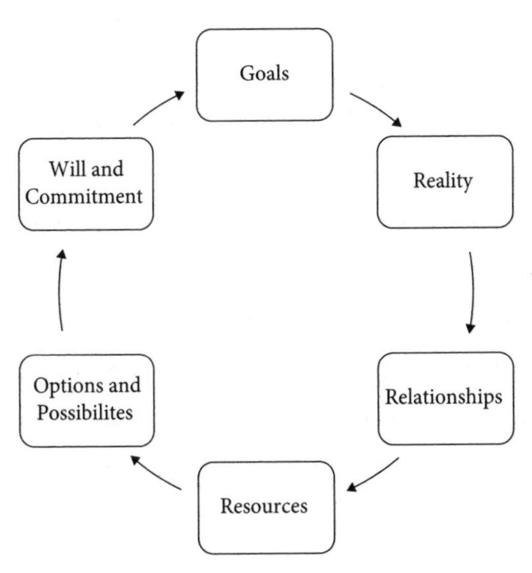

FIGURE 13.2 ***GRRROW model (adapted from Sir John Whitmore).***

Managers are often tempted to skip over the goals and go directly to reality questions. Typically, managers are very good at asking analytical questions concerning reality, but are not so good at asking about the emotional and psychological realities. As for options, the trap that many managers fall into is to give *their* options and opinions rather than ask the coachees for theirs. Many people also forget to ask about will and commitment, assuming that it will just somehow happen! It is important to ask specific questions about the degree of will and commitment, to fix specific actions and dates and to follow up on these.

Appreciative coaching

This is based on a bigger theory called Appreciative Inquiry – it is nicely summarized by Gervase Bushe of Simon Fraser University in Canada. According to Professor Bushe, 'Appreciative Inquiry advocates collective inquiry into the best of what is, in order to imagine what could be, followed by collective design of a desired future state that is compelling, and thus does not require the use of incentives, coercion or persuasion for planned change to occur'. Based on this we suggest that when using Appreciative Coaching you can build the following structure for your team coaching:

- Inquire not into the team's failings, but into their strengths and resources, perhaps helping them to integrate any positive experiences and feedback they may already have.

- Help the team imagine a better future or desired state. Get them to visualize their preferred future and share it.
- Then help them work through the actions and behaviours they need to put in place in order to achieve the desired outcomes.
- Finally, ensure that you review how the team is progressing in its goals and objectives.

Solution Focused coaching

There are some basic assumptions and principles underlying the Solution Focused (SF) approach to coaching:

- The team has all the necessary resources to change.
- Change is happening all the time, so the coach's job is to identify and amplify useful change. The coach therefore needs to inquire where useful change has already taken place within the team.
- There is no one 'right' way of looking at things: different views may fit the facts just as well. The coach's role here is to challenge assumptions and perceptions.
- Detailed understanding of the 'problem' is usually little help in arriving at the solution. The coach does not have to spend huge amounts of time trying to

understand the issues in great detail. Rather his or her job is to ask good open questions in order to help the team reflect on and become more aware of their issues.

- No 'problem' happens all the time. There are always times when the problem is NOT happening, so a useful way forward lies in identifying what is going on when the problem does not occur. Again, the coach's role is to probe into when things are going well rather than when they are going badly. This can be unexpectedly difficult, as the teams are often focused on the problem and find it difficult to turn their attention to what is positive.
- Small changes in the right direction can be amplified to great effect. There seems to be a desire within organizations to effect big changes, but big changes are hard to achieve in reality. The SF approach stresses the importance of recognizing and encouraging when the team is taking small steps that are going in the right direction.
- It is useful to have the team imagine what a preferred future might look like. This takes the form of the so-called Miracle question where the coach asks the team (or individual team members) to imagine they have

> gone to bed and woken up the next day and a miracle has happened. Then the coach asks them to describe what is now happening. This can be quite a difficult technique, as often the coachee can resist the question and say that it is too difficult to answer, or become defensive and say that a miracle can't possibly happen! Nevertheless, it's worth persisting and getting the coachee to use their imagination and visualize their preferred future. Once they have done this, it becomes more possible for the team member to start describing the specific behaviours they could display in that future.

In the Solution Focused approach, it isn't necessary to delve into the roots of the problem or analyse the problem in detail. The focus, as its name suggests, is towards developing solutions and, in particular, the team's own solutions. This is achieved through a variety of steps and processes that first involve finding the **Platform** – what are we here to do today? Then you can move to **Counters**, which means asking about the coachee's strengths and resources. What do they have that will help them overcome their issue? Then you would ask **Scaling** questions – in other words, where are they on a scale of 1 to 10, with 10 being high? If, for example, the coachee says they are a 3, then you can ask where they would like to be? What would it be like if they were at 5? What would they be doing? Saying? Feeling? Then you would move on to asking about what small steps the coachee could take in the right direction and then give some positive affirmations to the coachee, before perhaps asking them to try out a different way of doing things before your next session.

Team coaching

One of the most common types of team performance is in sports where teams feature heavily; even if the sport is an individual one like tennis, there is still a team supporting the individual performer. Are there any transferable principles from team performance in sport to team performance in organizations? We believe so. Ashridge has worked with many sports teams and coaches over the years and we will share our thinking with you; we will also share ideas from sports coaches, managers and specialists with whom we have discussed these issues.

According to European, Commonwealth and World Champion sprinter and hurdler Kriss Akabusi, the difference between individual coaching and team coaching is that the team coach would do the same as the individual coach, but on top of this, would also need to look at areas like team strategy, team processes, systems and tactics.

As there might be less time for personal coaching in the team, team coaching should be more about processes and less about individual feelings and emotions. There may be an assumption in the team that each individual already has a personal coach. The team coach would be looking at the individual's role in the team's purpose, strategy and goals. So in the team you need to be on the same page and heading in the same direction. As Kriss puts it – 'It's less about me and more about us'.

Transferable learnings

A key question then is what are the transferable principles from team coaching in sport, to team coaching in businesses and organizations? According to research by Dr Mark Lowther of Cardiff Metropolitan University's School of Sport, there are three key transferable principles of team coaching. These are Context, Processes and Contact.

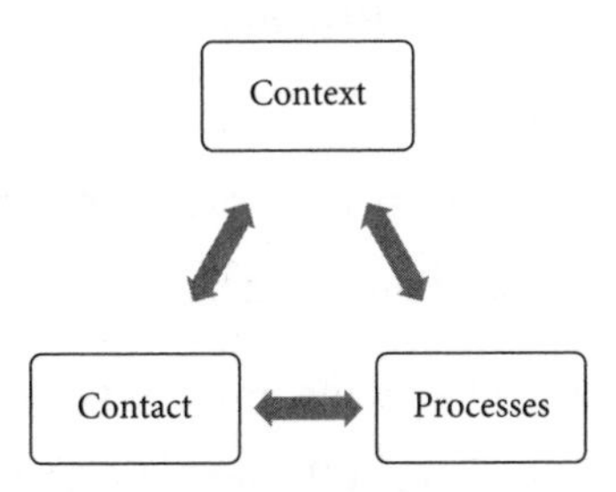

FIGURE 13.3 ***Transferable principles.***

Context

This is about the wider climate in which both the team and individuals operate. It is essential to create a culture and climate that encourages and supports the goals of the team. Former England Rugby head coach Stuart Lancaster used to say that culture preceded performance, and that if the culture was wrong, then performance would suffer. But the problem with this is the fact that a good culture doesn't necessarily create good performance. Yet the most successful sports team on the planet –the All Blacks – did have to address the culture of their team in order to create better performance. The critical question is, does the culture stand in the way of effective performance? If the answer is yes, then it needs to be addressed. This is the same in business as it is in sports organizations. The team leader needs to reflect on the existing culture within his or her team, and create the appropriate cultural climate in order for the team to perform effectively.

Process

This is about developing a cohesive team and the processes that can be used to do this. There are three subcomponents of process – Relays, Relationships and Shared Purpose.

- **Using Relays.** One of the processes is to be able to use senior members of the team to act as a relay. If the team is large, then you cannot realistically know

> what's going on with every member of the team. But the team members themselves can and do. If you are able to have a subgroup of senior team members who are on side with your vision and approach, then they can act as substitute team managers and coaches in the sense that they will remind team members of the team goals, values and ways of working and reinforce the key messages. This is common in highly effective teams in the world of sport. For example, the former Liverpool FC and Scotland footballer Graeme Souness (*Sunday Times*, 18 January 2015) agrees that the idea of having the senior members of a team act as a sort of relay is critical. He writes, 'When I was at Liverpool the coaches very rarely had to say anything because the senior players would set the standards for everyone else'.

As a team coach you cannot do everything, and unless you have senior members of the team, who are respected, relaying your approach it will be difficult to manage a team effectively. The New Zealand rugby team, the All Blacks, the most successful team on the planet with a win ratio of 85 per cent, also use this idea. They have a leadership group within the team, composed of the captain and senior players, who role-model and embed the values on a day-to-day basis. The point is that the coach is not enough. So when you look at your team, who are the team members who are respected and can relay your message? This is especially important when the team is dispersed geographically.

- **Relationships** – Another important aspect for the team coach to look at is the relationships between team members. For example, what is the level of trust between team members? What are the differences between team members; for example, what are the differences in ways of working, ages and expectations? Kriss Akabusi thinks that trust is critical. So what is the level of trust between you and the team and between team members themselves? As Kriss says, why would you listen to someone you don't trust or respect? So you may like to ask your coachees how much they are trusted by the team and follow that on with an exploration of how trust can be further developed in the team. See Chapter 7 for more on trust.
- **Shared purpose** – '*Talent without unity of purpose is a hopelessly devalued currency*' Sir Alex Ferguson, Former Manager, Manchester United Football Club (*The Independent*, 30 April 2011). It's critical to have conversations with the team about the shared purpose. This is not something that can be assumed, so there

> needs to be absolute clarity around that shared purpose. What does the team want and how will it get there? As a team coach it's your job to initiate and facilitate these conversations. If you don't, then you are likely to find that despite talented individuals the team is always going to be less than the sum of its parts. In fact you may find that the different individuals are working at cross-purpose to each other and actually sabotaging what you are trying to achieve.

These are issues that the team coach has to be aware of and has to bring to the surface as they are very often ignored.

> *The best results come from me following a process and the person being coached not being aware of the process.*
>
> Nigel Melville, Director, Professional Rugby, RFU.

Contact

It is about managing individual talent. Although we are talking about coaching teams, we can't lose sight of the fact that the team is composed of individuals, and so paradoxically perhaps, we need to be able to address the individual needs, issues, preferences and talents in the team. It is important not to lose sight of the individual and their unique personality traits and personal circumstances. While traditionally the focus of coaching was always about the team, the reality and complexity of modern group settings and squads require a leader to both skilfully coach the team and actively connect to the player. Dave Brailsford of British Cycling and Team Sky calls this a rider-centred approach.

At the same time, we need to be aware of team goals and any potential clashes between individual goals and team goals. So you need to be flexible to individual needs within the team and adapt your style to the needs of the team members. There is a popular saying – 'There is no I in team', and this has been widely accepted. But writer and researcher Dr Mark de Rond from Judge Business School at Cambridge University tells us that this is totally wrong and that there is in fact an 'I' in team. You have to address the individual components of the team as well as the team itself; otherwise, the team will not function effectively.

Team coaching – the five disciplines

Peter Hawkins of Henley Business School has developed a useful and practical model focusing on three aspects and five disciplines of team coaching. At the heart of the model are three essential aspects of the team:

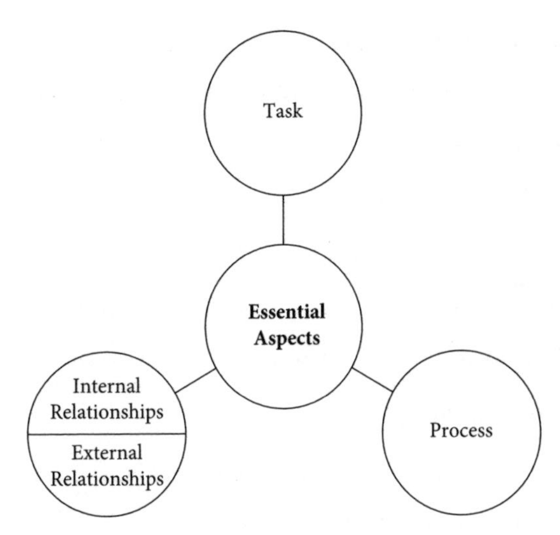

FIGURE 13.4 *The essential aspects of a team.*

- Task – the purpose of the team.
- Process – how the team will achieve its purpose.
- Relationships – this is looked at from two perspectives, internal and external.

Around these three aspects, Peter has developed five key disciplines. For each of the five disciplines he suggests some useful questions you can ask when coaching a team.

- **Commissioning**
  - Who does the team serve?
  - What is its purpose?

    - Why does it exist?
    - How does this align with organizational objectives?
- **Clarifying**
    - What is its collective task?
    - What are the core objectives?
    - Is the team clear about roles? Preferences?
    - Is the team clear about working processes?
- **Co-creating**
    - How is the team working together? How creative? How skilled at working together?
    - How does it partner internally?
    - How does it manage team dynamics?
- **Connecting**
    - How does the team partner with the wider system and your key stakeholders?
- **Core Learning**
    - How does the team learn?
    - How does it continue to learn?
    - How does it develop as a team?

We suggest that you use these questions together with your own personalized questions to create better awareness of the essentials of team performance in the context in which you are operating.

Challenges of team coaching

Nigel Melville, the director of Professional Rugby for the English Rugby Football Union, thinks that team coaching is more challenging than coaching individuals, as there are more parts and so many different personalities. Although he finds team coaching more challenging, he also finds it more rewarding than just coaching individuals. For him, the biggest challenge in the workplace is that it's often easier to fall into the trap of telling someone what to do rather than encourage them to work it out for themselves. On the sports field, the players have to do it themselves, so just telling them is not enough – you can't do it for them!

Another challenge is actually finding time to coach the team. Nigel suggests that it's essential to make time to coach. He recognizes that this is difficult. There doesn't seem to be any time to practise (as you would do in sport), because in business all the focus is on the next deadline, the next deal or the next meeting. No doubt you have experienced the same issues as Nigel. So how can you make sure that you set aside enough time for coaching the team?

His suggestion is you need to either slow down the pace of the work or develop a quicker coaching process that works for you. If not, you will not be an effective team coach, and your team's performance will suffer.

Key points from this chapter

- Remember that it's about getting the balance right between the team's needs and the individuals' needs.
- Remember the three key principles:
    - Context – make sure the climate and culture around the team is right.
    - Process – use trusted team colleagues as relays. Ensure the relationships between you, the team and the team members themselves are good. Think about levels of trust.
    - Contract – don't forget the individual.
- Successful team coaching builds trust and respect and helps develop peak performance.
- Make time to coach; don't become obsessed solely with action and results.

14

Managing challenging behaviour

The way a team plays as a whole determines its success. You may have the greatest bunch of individual stars in the world, but if they don't play together, the club won't be worth a dime.

GEORGE HERMAN RUTH JR., BETTER KNOWN AS BABE RUTH, THE AMERICAN BASEBALL PLAYER

In our work, and in life in general, we all have to deal with situations and people that we find challenging. By challenging behaviour, we do *not* mean situations where people ask challenging questions and become involved in a lively debate. What we mean is situations where people display unacceptable or disruptive behaviour that presents challenges to the processes and practices of the team. This chapter is about those people who exhibit disruptive or dysfunctional behavioural patterns.

This can cause you and your team members to take your eye off the performance ball in order to cope with and deal with the behaviour in question. When faced with this sort of challenging situation, your single most important role is to deal with the issue as speedily as possible so that it does not escalate. The success of any team has much to do with the way in which team members interact, as well as the team's overall cohesion and ability to get on with each other.

We will identify some of the most common challenging behavioural patterns experienced by people working in teams and suggest ideas for managing and dealing with difficult and dysfunctional behaviour. Before we begin to explore this area, let's look at some of the reasons for and implications of difficult and dysfunctional behaviour.

Challenging team members: Reasons and implications

Leading, managing and working in any team will be challenging at the best of times. What you do not want to happen is for people to display difficult behaviour. Most of us will have at some point in our lives have experienced teams where individuals or even groups of individuals have displayed behaviour that is challenging and dysfunctional.

For instance, one of the managers attending one of our leadership courses told us about an individual in his team who was sabotaging the team by talking about people in a negative way behind their backs. The issue here was that the individual concerned contributed at group meetings and appeared positive, committed and pleasant. However, he would often not deliver on promises, lied about his contributions and worst of all spoke about other team members behind their backs.

Patrick Lencioni (2002) identifies five dysfunctions that contribute to why teams struggle:

- absence of trust.
- fear of conflict.
- lack of commitment.
- avoidance of accountability.
- lack of attention to results.

Effective leadership and team development will work towards building an environment where trust, commitment, accountability and results orientation are present as well as ensuring that conflict is recognized and dealt with. However, our experience suggests there are still times when teams and individuals within these teams can become disengaged, disillusioned and demotivated and it is at these times that dysfunctional and difficult behaviour begins to manifest itself. Some of the most common reasons for this are:

- Personality clashes between team members, with the team leader or possibly with external stakeholders.
- When new team members join the team, and especially when time has not been devoted to integration – this can be a common occurrence in today's complex and busy working environment.
- People not committing to the team's work and therefore not pulling their weight – sometimes known as 'social loafing'.
- Misunderstandings between people, often due to not working face-to-face. Again, this is another common issue, particularly with virtual teams.
- Organizational changes such as new ownership, mergers or acquisitions, any of which can create uncertainty and fear, and which can result in people acting out of character.
- Changes to work processes and procedures that can cause people to feel loss of control or fear of failure.

Much of the above can be anticipated and planned for by keeping in touch with your team and building and developing an open and trusting working environment. Spend time communicating with your team to check how they are coping and feeling about any changes that are occurring, or simply when you observe any changes in behavioural patterns. This will enable you to plan a course of action to move things back to equilibrium.

Common challenging behaviours

We have identified nine of the most common types of challenging behaviour. These are all based on our own observations, together with stories told to us during our research interviews with people in a variety of team types from business, medicine, sport and the arts. The diagram below identifies the behaviours that people tend to display – the so-called challenging or difficult behaviours. You must always bear in mind that these behaviours are often played out in a less extreme way on a day-to-day basis. The problem arises when behaviour becomes more pronounced, extreme or overdone. For instance, people do not become pessimistic overnight. They tend to have this feature as part of their personality but under normal circumstances will manifest as an individual who is perhaps a bit of a worrier and who requires reassurance and this will be manageable when things are working well for them. However, when they feel threatened, fearful or pressurized for any reason, that behaviour can be displayed in more negative and extreme ways. This may be the case for each of the types we have identified.

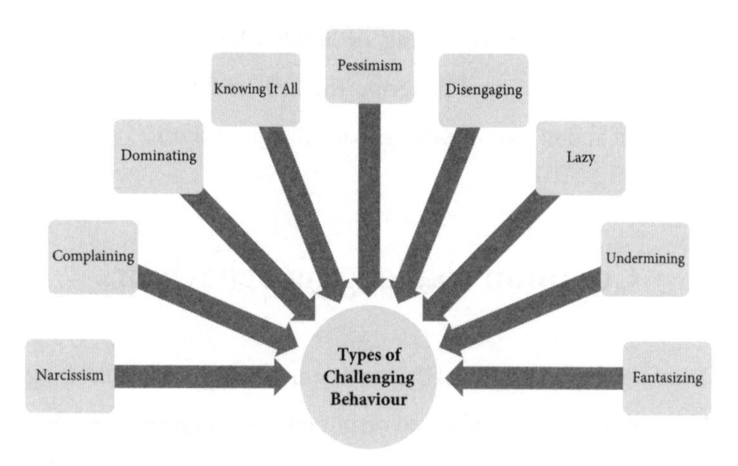

FIGURE 14.1 *Challenging Behaviours.*

Let's look at each of these challenging behavioural patterns and explore how they are displayed when dysfunctional. We will also offer ideas about how you can deal with these challenging types. Use this information to reflect about the various teams you lead or are a member of, and the characters in them, whether you can recognize any of the challenging types described below or indeed other challenging types you may encounter.

Narcissism

When things are going well, people who display this tendency can be highly energetic, focused and assertive; however, they can also lack empathy, are self-absorbed and can be exploitative. In a team environment, when things don't go their way, narcissistic behaviour can lead to overly competitive, argumentative and aggressive behaviour, all of which can be disruptive to the team.

Complaining

The person who always sees the negative side of things. We probably all know people like this; they just can't help themselves and seem to enjoy being discontented, which, when left to fester, can affect the morale of the whole team.

Dominating

When this behaviour is used effectively it can come across as self-confident, direct and action-oriented. But when people abuse this approach, it can also dominate conversations, intimidate and bully others to their way of thinking.

Knowing it all

People who know absolutely everything, always have an answer, have been everywhere and always have an opinion. These are annoyances but the real irritators are that this behaviour will be rather overbearing and dismissive of others' ideas.

Pessimism

Pessimists tend to see the worst in everything, will criticize new ideas and have a tendency to think of the glass in terms of 'half empty' rather than 'half full'. Used occasionally, pessimism can be a counter-balance for over-optimism and ambition. However, constant pessimistic behaviour can drag down the whole team, especially in challenging times.

Disengaging

This type of person is someone who displays apathetic behaviour and has lost interest in the people and work of the team. Any contribution at team meetings will tend to be either negative or cynical.

Lazy

This type of person has the skills to do the job but is simply too idle, lacking drive and energy.

Undermining

This behaviour is subversive, stirs up trouble between team members and undermines the team leader behind their back.

Fantasizing

This type of person has a tendency towards exaggeration, daydreaming, embellishment and elaboration of their experiences and ideas.

The common theme that runs through all of these challenging behaviours, if allowed to perpetuate, is the ability to affect the morale, energy and productivity of the team. This is one of the main reasons why challenging behaviour must be dealt with quickly.

Dealing with challenging behaviours

The first step is to determine whether the behaviour is occasional or a regular occurrence. If the behaviour is one-off or occasional then you should talk to the person to find out what's going on for them at the moment. Sometimes people display dysfunctional or unacceptable behaviour when things are going wrong for them, causing them to feel stressed or under pressure. This could be within the team itself, possibly some interpersonal issues between team members, or it could be caused by work in general. For instance, the work no longer challenges them or has become too challenging. Issues at home or in a person's social life can also impact their behaviour at work. A simple inquiry to understand what is causing the behavioural change may be all that is necessary – for instance, *'I have noticed that in the last few days you seem to be less less optimistic than usual; is something bothering you?'* In this example, you have noticed the behavioural change, you have reflected it back to the person and inquired as to what's happening. At this stage it is important not to judge, but simply to inquire. The awareness that their behaviour is having an affect on others may be sufficient to make the individual reflect and adapt.

On the other hand, if the behaviour is more deep-seated and part of the individual's normal way of operating, then it is important for you to deal with it both speedily and effectively. This in itself can be quite a challenge, as the individual may not be aware of the impact they are having on the team or that others perceive their behaviour negatively. Some people will be surprised and willing to work things out, while others may be trickier, especially when the behaviour is part of their normal work personality. Let's first explore what you can do with the people who you believe would be willing to change.

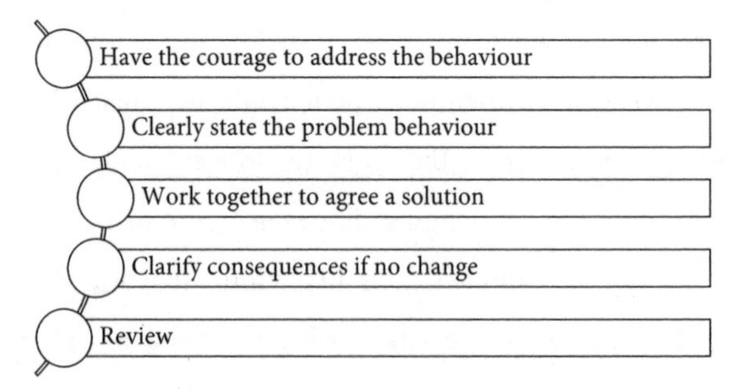

FIGURE 14.2 ***Process for dealing with challenging behaviour.***

Have the courage to address the behaviour

Many managers we work with talk to us about the difficulty they had when it comes to confronting a colleague's challenging behaviour. It is important for effectiveness as a leader to tackle the individuals and the behaviour that is causing the issue within the team. Both respect and empathy are important here, as well as confidence in stating the purpose of your discussion.

Clearly state, with evidence and examples, the behaviour that is causing problems

Don't prevaricate; get straight to the point. Preparation will help you to achieve this. You might want to write notes as a prompt to ensure you remain on track and also to reflect on the responses you may get from the individual in question. Talking about the sort of positive contributions the person has made in the past, or has the potential to make, can also be useful in helping them recognize that they do have the capability to contribute in a positive and effective way.

Work together to agree a solution

This will improve the level of commitment from the individual involved. Ask the person to reflect on what you have told them about their behaviour, how it affects the team and if they have any ideas to resolve the issues. During this process you should be exploring how the person likes to work, what motivates them and how you can help them to channel their energy so that they can contribute more effectively in the team. Once you have agreed solutions, then develop a plan and set benchmarks of success – these measures should be both achievable and observable.

This is important, as it must be noticeable to the other team members that something has changed. Making the individual accountable for any changes will also add to the effectiveness and commitment for the long term.

Clarifying and vocalizing the consequence of no change is also imperative

Challenging behaviour can be corrosive and affects the whole team often in a negative way. So make the individual aware that the current behaviour is not acceptable, and if changes do not occur, then further consequences will be inevitable.

Review

It is also worthwhile for you to review how you dealt with this situation so that you can learn from the experience and build your learning about handling similar situations in the future.

Finally, there may be occasions when you will come across people who demonstrate difficult and dysfunctional behaviour that constantly infects everyone around them, and eventually creates a toxic environment. When confronted, this type of person is often unwilling or possibly unable to change, especially if their behaviour is entrenched. If you are unlucky enough to come across such a person, then you must have a strategy to cope. Sometimes it is as simple as parting company, or if this is not possible, then find a way to reduce the negative effect the behaviour has on the team. For instance, you as team leader may have to intervene early on when you notice things are going off track.

Working as part of a team is not for everyone and sometimes your role as a leader is about diagnosing and recognizing where your people can best be deployed to add value. Recognizing that an individual is more of an independent operator, who, given the opportunity, could contribute more working on their own is a legitimate part of your role. Be aware that just because someone is causing challenges in a team, it does not mean that they will automatically cause less challenge as an independent worker. The goal is to work with the individual to find out their true motivators, and set goals for achievement – including interpersonal ones. If they can channel their energy and capabilities to achieving, then you have a win-win situation for everyone.

Remember that in the long run, keeping someone around who may affect you and your team in a negative way is pointless for all concerned.

Key points from this chapter

- Challenging behaviour from an individual will affect the whole team if not dealt with speedily and effectively.
- People are often unaware that their behaviour is causing a problem, so it is important to talk to them and make them aware of the impact they are having on others.

- As a team leader you can nip challenging behaviour in the bud by keen observation and awareness of any behavioural changes, pointing them out and dealing with them quickly.
- A person's behaviour can be affected by changes in their environment that cause them to feel pressured or stressed, so spend time figuring out why the difficult behaviour is happening.
- The best teams are made up of a variety of different personalities. As a team leader, you must be sure that the difficulties or challenges are leading to dysfunctional and toxic behaviour, not simply people expressing themselves in different ways.

15

Dealing with conflict

In great teams, conflict becomes productive. The free flow of conflicting ideas is critical for creative thinking, for discovering new solutions no one individual would have come to on his own.

PETER SENGE, MIT SLOAN SCHOOL OF MANAGEMENT

Conflict and confrontation are facts of life. When people work together, there is difference – for instance, difference of opinion, difference in personality, difference in skills and difference in experience, as well as the more obvious differences of age, gender and nationality. It is these differences that can cause conflict to arise. Like Peter Senge, we believe that conflict when handled effectively can be productive and is often a key feature in well-functioning, high-performance teams. The challenge is how the various people, the team leader as well as the team members deal with the conflict. It is important to recognize and distinguish between healthy productive conflict and unhealthy dysfunctional conflict.

In any team situation, there are a multitude of possibilities for where, when and with whom conflict can arise. It need not only be within a team but between the team leaders and a team member (or between team members). For example, within a team of say six people there are thirty possible inter-relationships, all of which have the potential for generating conflict. Teams can also experience inter-team conflict, conflict with the organization or certain people within the organization; conflict can also arise with external stakeholders – customers, clients, suppliers.

Whatever the situation, and whatever the cause and whoever is involved, it is important for leaders and their teams to be able to recognize when conflict exists, to have the skills to understand the nature of the conflict and to have the ability to resolve it. Too many people in organisations turn a blind eye to conflict in the hope that it will go away. This is rarely the answer, as dysfunctional conflict seldom solves itself. Left to incubate, conflict tends to escalate into a much bigger issue than if it had been dealt with promptly and effectively when first identified or observed.

In this chapter, we will first explore specific issues about conflict in teams, the difference between productive and dysfunctional conflict, and the symptoms and signs of conflict. We will then move on to offer strategies and processes for coping with and resolving conflict.

Healthy vs. unhealthy conflict

Mention the word 'conflict' to many leaders and their teams and they immediately think about situations where, in general, the behaviours of those involved have been dysfunctional and unproductive and the outcome has been negative, whether that is in relation to work output or relationships. However, as Peter Senge, senior lecturer at MIT, points out (see quote above), conflict can be productive when it encourages discussion, debate and creativity. One example of healthy conflict is where team members disagree about ideas for developing a new process for greater efficiency at work. This sort of disagreement (or conflict of ideas) can lead to improvement in the outcome when all parties involved share their ideas and then move forward in service of the overall goal. Of course, this requires the leader and the team to have a clear goal to work to and then to adopt a process that enables all parties involved to share their ideas and explore the best possible outcomes. It sounds easy but it does require you to have in place good principles and processes for resolving conflict.

How can you recognize healthy and unhealthy conflict? The following chart suggests some of the cues and clues we have observed.

Healthy conflict tends to involve	Unhealthy conflict tends to involve
• Task-focused issues • Respectful debate exploring identified problems • Genuine difference of opinions • Differing values or perspectives on an issue	• Personal attacks • Blame being attributed • Anger • Manipulative or patronizing behaviour • Win/lose situations

The first stage when dealing with perceived conflict is to determine whether or not it might be classed as healthy or unhealthy. As a team leader, it still falls to you to help people to work through the issue if it is healthy conflict or alternatively to help resolve the issue if unhealthy conflict. Later in this chapter, we will outline a process to follow.

Symptoms and signs of potential conflict

Recognizing the symptoms and signs of conflict can help you to diagnose and deal with conflict early. The visible signs of conflict – personality clashes, anger, arguments between people, development of win/lose situations – are relatively easy to spot. It is the less obvious symptoms and signs that you must be aware of. As a team leader it may be that you observe or sense some changes in the normal behaviour or way of working within your team. Picking up on these signs can be challenging as they can be very subtle and will require you to be familiar with what's normal for the team and for the individuals within it.

As a starting point, you may find it useful to reflect on your own behaviour when in conflict and what it is that causes you to move into your conflict zone. Reflect back over the past few weeks/months and identify a time when you have felt conflicted at work. Can you identify what it was that made you feel this way? Think about the specific situation: who was involved, what was said, what you felt, what you thought, what you did and what specifically pushed you to feel in conflict. By understanding your own behaviour when in conflict, and being more self-aware of the changes in your own conduct, you can better appreciate the changes that others go through. However, as we have already established, the cause of conflict and the changes that ensue are different for each of us. The important issue here is for you to recognize that behavioural changes can be an indicator of people moving out of their comfort zone and into conflict.

One theory that we find very useful to help people understand what tips them into conflict is 'Relationship Awareness Theory', which was developed by Dr Elias H. Porter. Part of his theory suggests that conflict happens when something important to you is threatened, which in turn compromises your self-worth. This is often related to the values you hold, and of course this can be different for different people. When we do a deep dive conversation with managers and leaders about conflict, we have found that very often they identify the following issues that can act as triggers:

- Competence being challenged.
- Others being patronizing, dismissive or aggressive.
- My rights as an individual being challenged.
- Someone being personally hostile.
- Overly emotional behaviour by others.
- Being exploited by someone.
- Dealing with intractable personalities.
- Being ignored.

Any of these feelings, if not recognized, can result in escalation towards conflict. The other interesting part of Porter's theory is that people do not usually move straight from effective behaviour to conflict behaviour. He suggests that we tend to go through a process of movement over a period of time. This time period can be very short, with changes happening rapidly, or it can happen over a very long period. If you want to know more about this theory and how it works in practice, you may find it useful to complete the Strength Deployment Inventory, which is the questionnaire Porter developed based on his theories. Information on this can be found at www.personalstrengths.uk.

Recognizing the symptoms and signs of conflict can in some cases be easy. For instance, loud arguments between team members, when you are cc'd into irate emails from team members or other stakeholders, maybe at a team meeting when colleagues become entrenched, rivalry between teams that becomes unhealthy, or even when you are dealing with a poor performer who has difficulty accepting your feedback.

Some visible signs of conflict are more obvious – for instance, increased absences and sick leave. However, other more subtle indicators of conflict or potential conflict may be less clear. For instance, the following are all examples of the sorts of subtle behaviour changes you may notice:

- When you observe subtle changes in behaviour within the team
    - Less general chit-chat.
    - Increased periods of silence.
    - Some team members not engaging with others.
- A general feeling of poor morale in the team.
- Team members' levels of motivation dropping.

LESSON FROM BUSINESS

EXAMPLE OF CONFLICT BEING TRIGGERED

This example was shared with us during a discussion with a colleague. (We have changed the names to ensure confidentiality.)

Susan was a member of a team of management consultants who tended to work independently and only came together occasionally for team reviews. It was at one of these events that the conflict happened. Susan explained to us that she knew she had a short fuse towards a couple of her colleagues in the team, based on her previous experience of their behaviour at such meetings. The behaviour she talked about was cynicism, patronizing behaviour towards others, and general lack of respect for other team members. She felt the people in question only attended such meetings to stir things up.

On this occasion Susan was chatting with a couple of her colleagues when Jim arrived in the room and made a beeline for her group and sat down. His opening remarks on joining them were, 'Well, here we are again. Another complete waste of a day'. Susan immediately snapped – she said to Jim, 'If that's how you feel then why on earth stay? Why not just go now and save us all a lot of grief having to put up with your whining and cynicism'. Jim then got up and walked out!

Susan went on to explain that she felt terrible afterwards, as she hadn't meant for this to happen. She simply wanted Jim to realize that his behaviour wasn't helpful. She did, however, realize that her reaction had been aggressive and confrontational. During our discussion we went on to explore her reaction and she realized that lack of respect shown to others was a major conflict trigger for her.

This type of conflict is quick and usually ends in a relationship breakdown – which, in fact, it did in this instance. Susan also explained that she was surprised by her own response in this particular situation, and the speed of her reaction and anger.

We believe that as a team leader your ability to deal with conflict will be assisted by:

- Keen observation skills.
- Good knowledge of your team members' usual behavioural patterns and motivations at work.
- Recognizing changes and dealing with things early.
- Adopting a conflict resolution process that works for you.

What follows is a process that we have found useful in our work as tutors and consultants and also when managing our own teams.

Conflict resolution process

We offer the following seven-step process. This encompasses the stages necessary to diagnose whether or not the conflict is healthy or unhealthy and then a process to follow towards resolution. The very nature of conflict suggests that things are not flowing smoothly and therefore you may find that, in using this process, you have to flex it to suit the particular situation and the people involved.

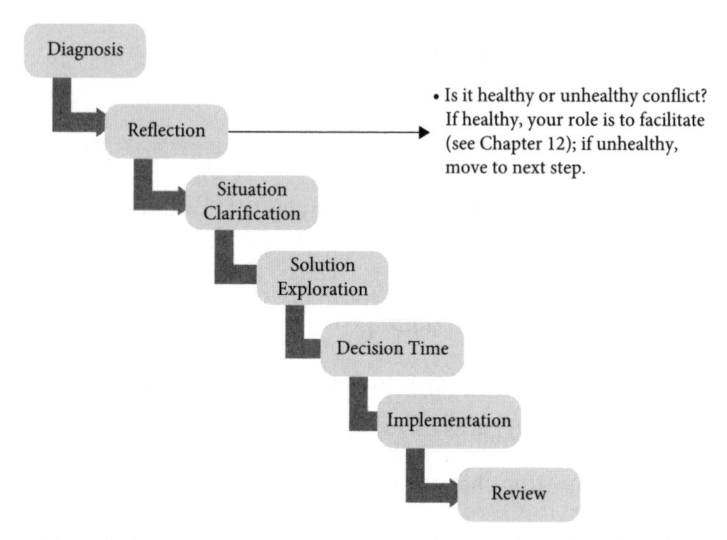

FIGURE 15.1 ***Conflict resolution process.***

Each of the stages in this process involves a range of skills, techniques and practices that can be used as described or adapted to suit your own situation.

Step 1 – Diagnosis – At this stage you have become aware that some disagreement, confrontation or other unusual behaviour is present within the team. The challenge here is to determine the extent of the disagreement, and whether or not it is simply a healthy debate or something that is escalating towards full-blown conflict. Observation is key at this point. Be clear whether what you are seeing, thinking and feeling indicates that there may be a conflict brewing. Focus on the issue and the people involved and establish how the situation arose by talking with all involved to identify the key issues.

Step 2 – Reflection – This is the stage where you must decide whether or not this is a case of healthy debate that you need to keep an eye on. If you feel it is simply a lively debate between co-workers, then your knowledge of the people involved and how they generally cope with debate and disagreement will be helpful. In addition, the topic of the disagreement may also have some bearing; for instance, the degree of freedom for the people involved to reach their own outcome. You may need to facilitate the process to help the disagreement to reach a healthy outcome or alternatively to move towards conflict resolution. If you feel you have to get involved, then you could use some of the suggestions for facilitating that were outlined in Chapter 12.

If, on reflection, you feel the situation is building towards, or is already a conflict, then you must intervene to ensure the issue reaches a satisfactory outcome and all parties involved understand that your primary role is to help them resolve the issue and move on. If this is the case, agree with all involved as to where and when you will meet to begin the conflict resolution process. You might also indicate how you intend to progress and that each person should be willing to talk about what's going wrong and come up with ideas for resolution in a professional manner. Your role is to work with them to resolve the issue, not to tell them what to do.

Step 3 – Situation clarification – In this step, questioning, listening, testing, understanding and clarifying are the key skills. Your role now is to be sure that you have a clear understanding of the conflict issue from the perspective of all the parties involved and without judgement. In essence, as the team leader (and assuming you are not involved in the conflict process yourself), your role is as a mediator to encourage those involved in the conflict to describe the situation as they see it. You should encourage open dialogue (face-to-face if possible), where each person involved explains their perspective, their thoughts and feelings about the issue and any ideas they have for moving forward. The important matter now is to encourage and enable those involved to talk openly about the conflict issue and for you to listen and understand so that you can help them towards a resolution that is acceptable for everyone.

Step 4 – Solution exploration – Once both you and those involved in the conflict feel that you have a clear understanding of the situation from all perspectives, then it is time to explore possible solutions or ways ahead. Sometimes you may find that during the previous stage you have begun to develop possible solutions and you may like to begin with these. Then, if necessary, brainstorm with others to help you further develop a range of options and possibilities. Your role here is to help to create ideas, to enable movement by all involved towards a mutually acceptable outcome.

Step 5 – Decision – Assuming you have effectively worked through the previous stages, all those involved should be beginning to appreciate each other's differing perspectives on the issue and recognize that the best way ahead is to move towards a mutually acceptable outcome. This should be something that everyone can accept and live with, and will often involve some degree of compromise. This stage should not be rushed, as it is vital to ensure that everyone understands the outcome. The important skills at this stage are clarity of language (to restate the decision), listening, clarification and summarizing. Make sure everyone involved has verbally agreed (and in writing if necessary) the outcome and that they understand the mutual benefits of what has been agreed. Failure to get this stage right can lead to a re-ignition of the conflict.

Step 6 – Implementation – Your role now is to observe the implementation process. This is the time when you must assess whether or not the conflict resolution process has been successful or not, by observing how the solution works in practice. Therefore, your skills of listening and observing are important to gauge if the people involved are willing to work together to ensure success.

Step 7 – Review – Dealing with any conflict resolution process is not easy. Conflict almost always involves compromise and concessions and will be an emotional experience for all. However, it can also be a good learning opportunity; therefore, it is worth reviewing the process to understand what worked, what didn't work and how you can build on this for the future. Conflict is a fact of life, so developing skilful ways of handling it will serve you well as a team leader.

Additional note for team leaders

Most of the above information suggests that you are not involved in the conflict yourself. If, however, you are involved, then much of the above will still apply. But you may like to involve someone else to act as mediator – either someone completely neutral, or perhaps your boss or another member of your team. Whoever it is, they must be acceptable to all parties involved.

Key points from this chapter

- Conflict and confrontation are a fact of life. The challenge is to determine whether it is healthy or unhealthy conflict and to diagnose how best to handle the situation.

- Team leaders must be on the lookout for the signs and symptoms of conflict and be willing to deal with conflict situations speedily and effectively.
- Recognizing and understanding your own and others' conflict triggers is a useful ability for team leaders to develop.
- Following a structured conflict resolution process will help you to work through any situations to an effective outcome.

16

Change in teams

Things do not change, we change.

HENRY DAVID THOREAU, AMERICAN WRITER

The Greek philosopher Heraclitus said that 'We can't step in the same river twice', implying that change is a constant companion. If this is the case, then as a team leader you need to be able to deal effectively with change, know how to initiate it, how to deal with resistance to it and how to understand the process of change.

It's also a paradox that although there is constant change, people tend not to like change and are resistant to it. This is especially – although not exclusively – the case when change is imposed upon you, or you *feel* that it is being imposed.

In this chapter, we will offer a range of ideas for initiating change, a process for change and for dealing with resistance to change.

Initiating change

The obvious thing to do when you have to initiate change is to try to involve the team in the process of change. If team members are involved in creating the changes and have a degree of ownership, then they are more likely to implement the desired changes and less likely to avoid or even sabotage the changes. Clearly, it is not always possible to involve the team in the entire process of change, but our experience of change initiatives shows us that it's almost always possible to allow people to have some degree of input into the process. The alternative is an exclusively top-down approach, which is rarely optimal.

How you frame the change is critical. American political scientist George Lakoff said, 'that frames trump facts', meaning that if a proposed change is framed in an ill-thought-out way, without full regard for the others who are involved, then it may be regarded by them in a negative way. Many initiators of change fall into the trap of giving insufficient thought to how the change will be perceived by others. There is a tendency for change initiators to simply state their case for change from their own perspective, with little or no involvement from the people who will have to implement the change on a daily basis! Those charged with making the change a reality (as opposed to those initiating the change) may therefore see the change as undesirable or ineffective, or both, and then will not be motivated to implement it effectively. They will frame the change as just one more attempt by top management to interfere in their jobs.

The most effective way to frame the desired change is to look at how it might actually be positive for those having to implement it. If this isn't possible – and often it's not – then another way to frame it is to look at the change from the perspective of the clients and show how the change will make life easier for them. You can then connect that to the continued success of the team or organization, and therefore of team members' jobs.

A process of change

There are many different models and theories of change. A model which resonates with us, and we find to be particularly effective when working with management teams, is William Bridges's model of change.

Bridges is best known for his transition model of change. For him, transition is the psychological process of adapting to change, and he identified three phases in transition:

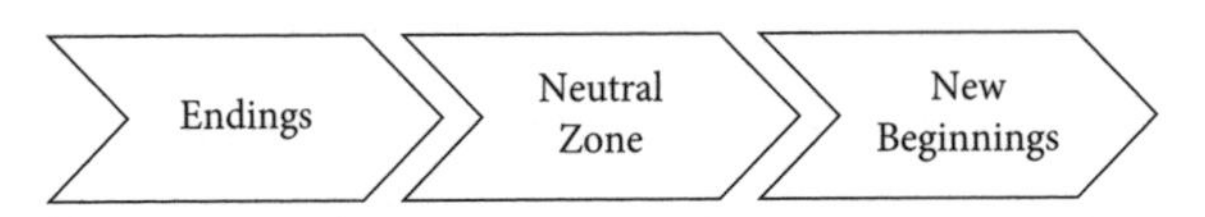

FIGURE 16.1 ***Transition Phases.***

- Endings – letting go of the past.
- The neutral zone or area of confusion.
- New beginnings – starting afresh.

Endings

This phase involves making sure that the past is over and it means letting go of the past. This is not easy and is often overlooked by those initiating change. There is a tendency for them to be thinking about the new beginning that is desired, rather than focusing on what those affected by the change are having to let go. But those affected by the change are much more focused on what they might be losing, than the new beginning desired by the initiators. So when planning a change, you need to try to establish what people are going to have to let go of, and point out to what extent things will actually remain the same. In essence, you are helping people to reframe what they are losing to what they are keeping. But you should also try to let people take some of the past with them – even if it's only something symbolic. Change initiators often overlook the emotional cost of change. You must recognize that there is real emotion involved for people who are letting go of something which was meaningful to them.

By helping people to let go of the past, understanding that they are maybe mourning the past and by being empathetic towards the emotions, you can make the transition much easier to accept.

One example of this from our consultancy experience is when a major multinational took over a local company. Two years later the workers on the shop floor were still wearing the overalls with the old company's logo. There was also lots of reference in conversation to 'the good old days', but in fact many things had changed for the better.

The neutral zone

It is defined as a period when people are still in confusion, and is seen as a necessary part of the change transition. In other words, you cannot move from Ending to New Beginning without going through this phase. At this stage, people have begun to understand what they are losing, but are not sure where they are going or what they might be gaining. Such confusion is normal and what is needed is support and encouragement, and perhaps some coaching and mentoring. If you have initiated a change, you have to understand that there *will* be confusion, even if you personally are clear about the need for and direction of change. Don't try to rush through this period, or you will find that the change is not fully accepted. Make sure you help, support and reassure people in this phase and keep communicating throughout. The big danger here is that your team will not share any feelings of confusion with you, and will attempt to hide it, perhaps through fear or embarrassment. But the fact that it might be hidden doesn't change the fact that it is there. People often leave a team or organization during this period, especially if it is not well-handled, and you could be at risk of losing some of your best people.

New beginnings

Once you have gone through the Endings and Neutral zones of change, you can then expect that people will really start to accept matters and will now have more energy and a renewed sense of purpose. However, this new beginning is a result of going through the process as described above, and cannot happen without some version of the process. It might take some people longer than others, and this is also normal. Certain people will be able to let go fairly quickly, and not spend too much time in the neutral zone, but other team members will take longer and will need more support. Remember that this is a normal reaction to change, so don't be tempted to rush the change process, or the change will not take hold effectively.

An example here is where one of our clients – senior managers of a large European energy company – thought they were already at the new beginnings stage. However, when asked, over 100 of their staff suggested that they were still in a confused state – the neutral zone. The senior manager had arrived at the new beginning stage, but they had omitted to bring their people with them through the process.

Resistance to change

There is frequently resistance to change initiatives within organizations, and we feel that this is largely because the change process is not handled well or for one of the following reasons illustrated below.

The usual process for instigating change is that someone decides to make a change, then hands down instructions without

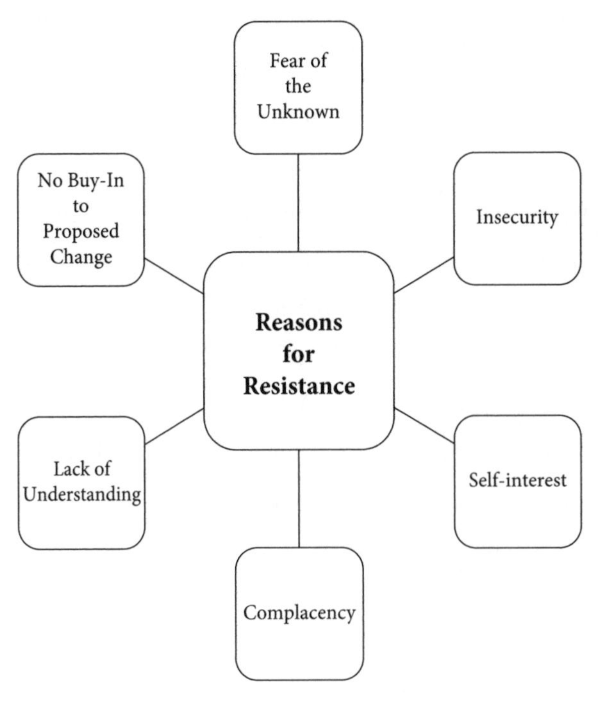

FIGURE 16.2 *Resistance to Change.*

first of all inquiring into the reality of the situation on the ground. The change is then felt to be more about the boss making his or her mark rather than a real attempt to change things for the better. If at all possible, we recommend a consultation period with the goal of finding out more about the realities of the situation.

Another common occurrence is that often when senior teams are initiating change they spend lots of time discussing and evaluating their ideas; during this time they are already moving throughout the change process. What they often forget is that when it comes to implementation, the people that have to do this have not yet begun to go through the process. It is vital that you communicate the change early so that others are given the opportunity to buy in to the change, and to begin moving through the change process. You must also present definite facts and irrefutable proof about the need for the change as well as evidence from clients, employees, etc., to show that you have been inquiring and listening. You still have to go through the three-stage process described above, but it should be an easier process than if the change is imposed from the top with no concern for the views of others.

Change implies that people go through a psychological process as well as a physical one. As a team leader and change agent, you will have to be aware of the emotions and potential resistance involved in any change process.

Key points from this chapter

- Change is as much an emotional process as a physical one.
- Make sure you understand what causes resistance to change.
- If you do not bring the people who are implementing the changes with you on the journey, then you have not really achieved effective change.

17

Dealing with politics in teams

Politics in organizational life is an everyday reality, yet many of us see political skill as a negative attribute. The reality, in our view, is that unless you are able to operate within a political landscape, you will not be as effective as you could be. As a team leader you would be wise to invest time and energy to develop your skills in this area.

The word 'politics' comes to us, via old French and Latin, from the Greek word *politicos*, which means concerning the city and the citizens. Its initial meaning was simply dealing with the matters that arise between citizens and their city. Over time, the meaning has changed somewhat. The *New Oxford Dictionary* defines politics as 'activities within an organisation that are aimed at improving someone's status or position and are typically considered to be devious or divisive'. There is now a somewhat negative perspective there. However, the *Collins English Dictionary* (2011) describes politics as 'The complex or aggregate of relationships of people in society, especially those relationships involving authority or power'. This brings us closer to the original meaning of the word, with fewer or no negative connotations.

It seems to us that the different perspectives offered by these two dictionaries are reflected in organizational life – with some people believing politics to be a normal part of organizational life and others seeing it as something to be avoided. Leadership guru Peter Drucker says that no leadership education is complete until it is grounded in the political realities of organizational life, and we think that it's vital that team members are at the very least aware of the politics that are going on, both internally to the team and externally in the wider organization.

Political awareness is largely about:

- Getting to know how things are done and having the skill to work with the informal organization.
- Being able to position yourself and your ideas to their best advantage.
- Having an understanding of who holds power and influence in the team and wider organization.
- Knowing how decisions are made and who makes them.
- Not taking things at face value, recognizing that you must sometimes read between the lines.

- Deploying your skills and abilities appropriately for the stakeholder group.
- Knowing who in your organization deals effectively with the political landscape and learning from them.

We wholeheartedly agree with Drucker's view that political awareness is a necessity for successful leadership. In fact, we would go even further and suggest that working with your team to help them get to grips with the political arena in the organization will enable your team to work more effectively. It is of course important to point out that it is very easy to become embroiled in organizational politics and to use them for individual gain – this will not serve you well in the long run.

The next important skill is to understand the political climate and recognize how best to work within it.

Power and politics

Power is intimately connected to politics in organizations, and the question of who has power, how they use it and how people can get it is a common theme. Power is usually defined as the capacity to direct or influence others or the course of events.

We find that many people are rather unaware of the different types of power that are available, and focus somewhat exclusively on one type of power – that is to say formal, positional power, also called legitimate power. In this case, that might be the power someone has as the team leader, although many team leaders in this age of matrix management and project working don't actually have any formal power! In any case, there is a definite tendency among organizations to move from competition to collaboration or from an 'I' to a 'we' focus. However, there are many other types of power available to both team leaders and team members, as illustrated below. Social Psychologists John French and Bertram Raven first described these forms of power in 1959.

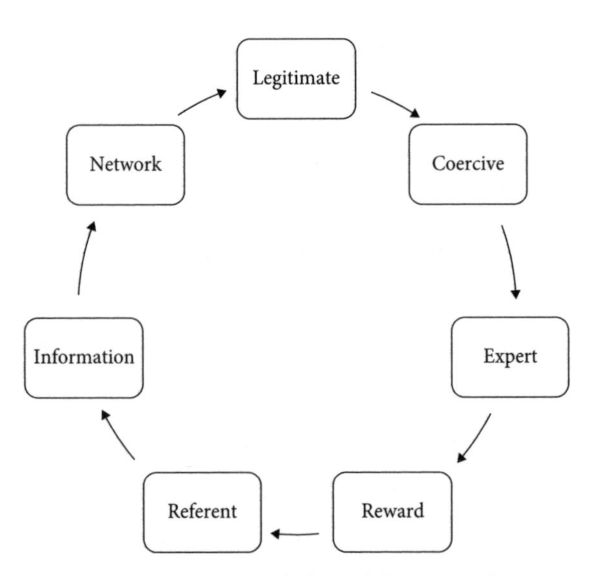

FIGURE 17.1 ***Forms of power (adapted from French & Raven).***

Legitimate power

It is bestowed by one's position in the hierarchy and is the formal power you have to tell people who report to you what to do within the scope of their contract with the organization. However, even though you have formal power, you cannot rely solely on it. Team members will accept a limited amount of legitimate power, but will also want to be influenced and convinced to do things, rather than simply being told what to do.

Coercive power

It uses threats and punishment to oblige people to do things, and we make the assumption that this is no longer desirable in businesses and organizational life. However, many commentators suggest that coercion still exists and is often applied in quite subtle ways.

Reward power

It is, as its name suggests, the power to reward people. This could be with money, for example, but could also be the power to give favours, open doors, etc.

Referent power

It is about people who are popular and therefore have power because of their character, and ability to attract and influence people. You could also call it charisma.

Information power

It is about who holds knowledge and information that can be used to get what they want or advance their own or their team's interests.

Network power

It is about connections and who you know. You may have very little formal or legitimate power in the team, but the excellent relationships and friendships you have both inside and outside the team and organization may well be a source of power. As the saying goes, 'It's not what you know but who you know!'

The important thing is to know what power is available to you in each situation, and to try and understand what power can be used by others in the team in order to lead and influence more effectively.

Understanding who has power, and what kind of power, becomes essential when you are trying to influence. For example, if you are bringing a new idea to a meeting, then you need to have pre-persuaded 51 per cent of the power in the room in order to have a good chance of success. That might be just one person or a combination of people, but you need to know where the power lies!

Key points from this chapter

- Without understanding the sources of power, you cannot deal effectively with the political environment in your organization.
- It is part of your role as a team leader to be aware of, and deal effectively with, the political environment in your organization.

18

Derailment

I have no spur to prick the sides of my intent, but only vaulting ambition, which o'erleaps itself and falls on the other.

WILLIAM SHAKESPEARE, *MACBETH*, ACT 1, SCENE VII

One of the key risks for you to be aware of as a team leader is the risk of derailment – for you or any team member. But what exactly is derailment? It means being knocked off the course that you and others expected you to follow in your career. It's about not achieving what you could have achieved. Studies by US researcher Morgan McCall and the Centre for Creative Leadership have shown that derailment is a common occurrence among high-potential managers in organizations. What happens is that the qualities that initially led managers to being on the fast track have a dark side, which potentially can knock them off course later in their career. It's very important to be aware of the potential derailers that could knock you, or individual team members, off track.

Some of the sources of initial managerial success are:

- **Good track record**, where people get excellent bottom line results, and have high impact in functional/technical areas.
- **Brilliance**, where managers were perceived as extremely smart and intelligent.
- **Commitment/Sacrifice** – managers who were seen as loyal to the organization, who were willing to work long hours and accept any assignments, no matter the cost to family life and health.
- **Charm** – people who were charming, but where the charm could be turned on and off like a tap. It was often used selectively when they needed something, or used upwards to their bosses and to those who make performance judgements.
- **Ambition** – people who actively sought out promotion and a leadership role, doing whatever it took to be successful.

Unfortunately these strengths and qualities can also have their negative sides. The strength first becomes overdone and then develops into a potential flaw. Let's look at the list of strengths and qualities again and identify some of the potential downsides.

- **Track record**

People may well have a good track record, but the issue is whether this might have been achieved in a very narrow area.

For example, if the success was in a technical area alone, it could have blinded people to the broader context of teamwork and leadership. Success may also have been achieved in destructive ways. Or perhaps the excellent track record was solely down to fortuitous events – like a rising stock market, for example – rather than the inner qualities of the person. Or perhaps other colleagues may have had more influence on the success than the person in question. For example, the success may have been due to a brilliant teamwork but the other team members were not given credit.

- **Brilliance**

It might seem an excellent thing to have brilliant people on the team, but that too has its downsides. Brilliance can intimidate others, and brilliant people can devalue people they see as less brilliant than themselves.

They can also devalue others' ideas and contributions because they are too egotistical. So if you are managing a brilliant person in your team, what can you do? Firstly pay close attention to how they interact and relate with others around them. Are they able to involve and listen to others? Can they bring other team members into the discussion and recognize the good ideas that others have? If they cannot do this, then you as team leader need to be able to step in and coach them on this, as they may be showing the initial signs of derailment.

- **Commitment**

At first glance it seems that high commitment is a good thing. But it too has its downsides. Over commitment can lead to defining one's whole life in terms of work and then expecting others in the team to do the same. It can lead to a manager being willing to do almost anything to succeed, including questionable or unethical activities. Managers who are too highly committed may then start to treat their team badly, and use their people as a means to securing their own personal targets. Although you probably don't want to stop people working hard, you might want to pay attention to your team members' work-life balance and ensure that they won't burn out, or, worse still, burn others out.

- **Charm**

The downside of charm is manipulation, which can be used selectively with people. Some people are able to switch easily between being charming when it can get them something, and being a bully. The people who behave like this are often capable of being charming one minute, then a dictator the next. If you do have someone in your team who uses charm a lot, make sure that they are actually being charming to most of the people, most of the time. Let's face it: they are probably going to be charming to you, their boss. So just make sure you know what's going on in the team when you are not there!

- **Ambition**

Ambition is good – but to be too ambitious is to risk overstretching oneself and the organization. Highly ambitious people can become *unrealistically* ambitious and end up taking on more than they can deal with. What you can also see are people who are overambitious and willing to do whatever it takes to achieve personal success, even at the expense of others, or indeed the team or organization.

All of this means that as an effective team leader you need to be aware of your own potential shadow side, in order to be able to manage it. It will also be important for you to be aware of the potential derailers that might affect your team.

Three dynamics of derailment

There are three key points that you need to remember when thinking about your team members' potential to be derailed. They are:

- Strengths can become weaknesses.
- Blind spots matter eventually.
- Success can lead to arrogance.

Strengths become weaknesses

Successful people can become arrogant and overconfident. It becomes difficult for people to abandon what worked in the past. So in some cases where the context and situation changes – for example, in a new job or department or in an overseas assignment – their strengths don't change and flex according to the context. They can then become inflexible, and so their decisiveness, for example, can turn into a weakness, and be seen as being dictatorial rather than decisive. Technical strength, for example, can lead to micromanagement, where instead of coaching and managing the team, you start doing the job yourself, and telling others exactly how to do it. Strong belief in principles can evolve into fanaticism or imposing one's beliefs on others.

One senior manager told us that some managers in his organization were so busy doing everyone else's job that they didn't do their own. This is an extremely common situation, where managers have been promoted solely on the basis of their technical knowhow and ability, yet they lack both relational and strategic skills.

This tendency is especially self-destructive when the people in the team actually know more about what they are doing than their boss does. This is a frequent occurrence. One manager in a large multinational company admitted that his weakness was his inability to step back and not interfere. Although his aim was to ensure success, his inability to let go was having the opposite effect. He didn't give his people a chance to step forward and take responsibility themselves and they ended up resenting him.

Sooner or later, if you are successful, you will end up managing people and functions outside of your area of expertise. When this happens, if you want to continue being successful, you have no choice but to step back and let go most of the time.

Blind spots matter eventually

We all have blind spots of course, but the fact is that if we ignore them and do not accept feedback, then they will catch up with us in the long run. None of us are perfect but the key thing is to become aware of our blind spots and be prepared to do something about them if they are potential derailers. For the team leader this is doubly complex. Firstly you have to be sure to avoid derailment yourself, and then be aware of the potential derailers that might affect your team members. As if that wasn't difficult enough, you then have to step in and manage that team member effectively.

One of these blind spots is being insensitive to others. According to the research this is the most common flaw among derailed executives and is the strongest differentiator. One senior team leader that Mike coached admitted that his drive and ambition had a social cost. It led to him sacrificing family time and social connectivity. He said that he could sometimes be 'brutal' and that he needed to learn how to be kinder, to himself, his family and his team.

Power and intimidation can of course produce compliance in the short term, but insensitivity to others can lead to lack of support at crucial junctures, failures of team members to pass on important information and loss of ideas from the team.

Success leads to arrogance or complacency

Arrogance can be present at all levels and is a key feature of derailment. Arrogance has special features – it grows over time, it creates a feeling of invincibility and blindness to one's impact and its potential consequences. Arrogance leads to over-optimism. Arrogant managers believe that expertise in one area makes them experts in others.

Arrogance also creates the belief that normal rules do not apply. A relentless pursuit of results, without regards for people or values, leads to temptation. A high degree of power over others, together with a track record of success, blinds many executives to the reality of their dependence on others. As we have seen, it's not possible to achieve success without others, so arrogance is ultimately self-defeating from the organization's perspective.

Preventing derailment

As a team leader, what can you do to prevent derailment? You might be wondering why people don't correct their weaknesses before they cause problems. The research tells us that there are several reasons. The main one is that the person has not yet been negatively affected by the weaknesses. We would add that they are perhaps not yet aware – or only partially aware – of those weaknesses. They refuse to admit to any weakness and disregard any information and feedback coming to them. They are, in effect, in denial. Their culture, whether national or organizational, may also play a part. So it is important that the person develops a high degree of self-awareness, and crucially that you as a team leader have the strength and energy to give feedback to such a person on your team. It's also essential that the organization itself has a robust enough culture to confront this denial, and that support and development – perhaps in the shape of coaching or mentoring – are available.

Learning and development is critical in the quest to prevent derailment. Unfortunately it is often overlooked in favour of action. If you stop to reflect and learn from a particular course of action, it is seen by many as a waste of time. So it is important that you take the time, with your team, to reflect and, above all, learn from events.

It is your job to make sure that you pick up on the signs of potential derailment in your team members, and that you have the skills to do something about them. The following guidelines might help.

Intervene

Don't do nothing. Have the courage to intervene and point out the consequences of people's actions.

Coach

Being a team manager implies that you need to be able to coach and develop your people. See Chapter 13 for more information on how to coach effectively.

Give regular feedback

Don't wait for annual appraisals. Make sure your feedback to team members is frequent so that you catch issues before they get out of hand. Learn how to give feedback effectively and skilfully.

Analyse

Analyse your own and your team members' strengths and weaknesses and list the potential flip sides of your strengths. Be honest with yourself and think about the implications of any overdone strengths.

Have a personal fool

In literature you will notice that many kings had fools, often called jesters – a servant who was allowed to criticize them, because no one else would dare to! Make sure you have a trusted colleague who can give you real and honest feedback. Encourage your team members to challenge you and to tell the truth.

Stop trying to control everything

Life is complex and uncertain and you can't control everything – so don't try to. Allow others space to take initiatives and learn to trust your team more.

Rely less on purely technical skills

Listen more, tolerate ambiguity more, get more feedback from colleagues and co-workers and external people as well as your boss.

Become more focused on problem-solving

Some managers seem to be focused almost entirely on promotion, rather than helping their team and solving problems. Although it is normal to want to progress, if you put your entire attention on it rather than doing the hard work that goes with it, you will be noticed and people will resent it.

Become more relationally aware and intelligent

We believe that relational intelligence is often overlooked. But the ability to connect emotionally and relate to other people is clearly essential to being an effective team leader.

Be aware of your interpersonal impact on others

Get feedback often. Be prepared to admit to any mistakes, be humble enough to apologize for them and make sure you learn from any mistakes.

You should be aware of your own potential derailers, and also those of your team members. Here is a short exercise, which you can do with your team, to help you reflect about your own, and your team's potential for derailment.

List five strengths that you believe have led to your success so far:

1	
2	
3	
4	
5	

Can you see how these strengths can be or could become a weakness? If yes, then note the situations in which each of the above strengths could be overdone and potentially get you into trouble.

1	
2	
3	
4	
5	

Given that what you see as a strength may become an overdone strength, can you identify one or more of your strengths that you would like to manage more effectively?
Everybody has some weaknesses. What do you think are your most significant weaknesses?

1	
2	
3	
4	
5	

Reflecting over your weak areas, are there any that you have been given feedback on, from someone on the team or elsewhere? Put an asterisk beside it. What are the potential implications for these development areas? What specific actions can you take to modify your behaviour?

Key points from this chapter

- Not all people who derail show the signs described above, and not all people who do show the signs will derail.

- People who show several of the signs, over a long period of time, are at a much higher risk of derailment.
- Be aware of the fact that you as a team leader may have some of these potential derailers.
- Almost certainly some of your team members have overdone strengths that could derail them.
- Have the courage to step in and coach any team members who are in danger of derailing.
- If you ignore these overdone strengths or weaknesses or reward them, it sets the stage for future derailment.

AND FINALLY, THE FUTURE OF TEAMS

We believe that, looking ahead, effective teams will have an even more important role to play in the future of work. The hierarchical approach to organizational structure is fast becoming obsolete because it does not respond quickly enough to the changes in our VUCA world, where we now face so-called "wicked" problems on an ever more regular basis. Some of the influences that we see affecting the future are described below.

Impact of the millennial generation in organizations

It's interesting to look at both what Generation Y (those people born in the 1980s and early 1990s) and Millennials (those born up to 2002) want in terms of their jobs, careers and the type of relationship they want with their bosses.

Our research at Ashridge tells us that they want:

- Challenging /interesting work.
- A coaching and mentoring relationship with their boss.

- For their bosses to share their experience with them.
- A friendly relationship with their colleagues – in other words, no hierarchical relationships.
- Flexible working patterns.
- Public acknowledgement of their success.
- Technology-driven communication.

All these things are important and relevant for team leaders to be aware of, and act upon, if they want to get the best out of their Generation Y colleagues. Unfortunately, it seems that many bosses are resisting these needs, and are actually thinking more about what *they* want from their Gen Y team members. The critical question is, how do we help Gen Y and Millennials become the effective team leaders of the future?

Multi-generational teams

Teams will be composed of different cultures and different generations. The challenge for the team leader will be to assimilate these different cultures and generations into an effective team with shared values and purpose. We know that many of the Baby Boom generation (those born between 1946 and 1961) and those who follow will have to work longer, possibly into their

70s and 80s. Professors Lynda Gratton and Andrew Scott of London Business School have written a best-selling book about this subject called *The 100 Year Life* (published by Bloomsbury).

The challenge for the Baby Boomers in these multi-generational teams will be to adapt to new ways of working, new technology, new roles – such as coaching and mentoring – and the fact that they may report to people from a younger generation. The challenge for the younger generations tends to be more in relation to skill development – in particular the interpersonal, relational and leadership skills.

Holocracy

The term 'holocracy' was coined by Brian Robertson, who is the founder of Ternary Software in the United States. He was experimenting with more democratic forms of governance and distilled their best practices into a system that became known as holocracy. He published his book *Holocracy* in 2016. The website http://www.holocracy.org/how-it-works/ gives the essentials of this concept. We can summarize these as follows:

- Roles are defined around work, not people.
- Authority is distributed rather than delegated. Decisions are made locally and authority is distributed to teams.

- Changes are made to the organizational structure on a regular basis, but they are done in small and rapid iterations, rather than large-scale change.
- Rules are visible and transparent and everyone in the organization is bound by them, including the CEO.

Holocracy doesn't work for every organization, but its principles are, in our opinion, more in tune with contemporary working practices than traditional organizational practices. We believe that this system will influence many organizations, though it will not be adopted by all.

Team processes

We believe that the way teams work together and are led will need to change radically in the future. Instead of teams having a single leader who is in charge, every single team member will have to have the ability to both lead and to follow. This will require team members to become skilled in processes like facilitation and change. The world is changing far too quickly for us to be able to ignore the collective intelligence of the team. The founder of Action Learning, Reg Revans, told us that learning had to be equal to or greater than the rate of change in the environment. The environment is certainly changing quickly so we need to focus on our ability to learn.

Operating in different types and roles in teams

In the future, we will each have a network of teams to which we belong. According to research, only 38 per cent of companies are organized by function, so there will be more and more cross-functional, multi-cultural, virtual and multi-generational teams.

LESSON FROM THE MILITARY

Former army officer and Olympic athlete ***Dominic Mahoney*** *talks about the vital importance of training.*

No other teams train like the military. They spend 18–20 weeks a year in training, and the quality and intensity of training enable military teams to come together and perform very quickly. Training is seen as critical in the military, but how much training do we give our teams in organizations?

In both sport and the military, 80–90 per cent of time is spent training and preparing, so that when the time comes to perform, the performance is automatic. You don't need to think and reflect or get stressed, you just do it. But you can't 'just do it' without the appropriate training and preparation. Unfortunately, this is a common error in teams in business. So although it is impossible to spend as much time in training as in sport and the military, perhaps there is a need to spend more time in order to achieve that higher level of performance.

This will mean that we all have to develop our skills for working in different team types, with a variety of different kinds of people. Team leaders and team members will have to be skilful in their ability to collaborate, flex their style and relate to a wide group of people. In addition to this, it is becoming more common for reward systems to be much more team-based rather than individually based. This is a highly emotional area that will demand a step change in attitude and approach and will demand real skill on the part of the leader and the organization.

Engagement

Engaged teams work more effectively: research by Gallup shows us that engaged employees have 22 per cent higher productivity, 65 per cent lower turnover and 41 per cent fewer defects. The challenge for team leaders will be how to keep team members engaged. Some of the key behaviours for team leaders to demonstrate in this area are:

- communication
- listening
- valuing
- supporting
- empathy
- being target focused

- having a strategic vision
- showing active interest in the team members.

More teams

There will be more teams but they will be forming and disbanding more rapidly, so the skills required to create the team, help it get up to speed, perform effectively and then end it well will be at a premium. General Stanley McChrystal used the term 'a team of teams' to describe the new way of working he brought to the US military in the Gulf War. Harvard professor Amy Edmondson uses the verb 'teaming', to describe the fact that to work in a team is an active process. She also stresses the need for psychological safety in the team in order to allow team members to openly speak their mind. We believe that since teams will be *the* way of working, the aspects such as psychological safety will be important for the team leader to take into account.

Conclusion

All in all, there are a number of challenges facing teams, team members and team leaders. Those with a learning orientation and the desire and skill to collaborate effectively will find that working in great teams is rewarding and satisfying.

REFERENCES AND BOOKLIST

The Ashridge Management Index. 2012/13. Ashridge Business School.

Belbin Associates. 2009. *The Belbin Guide to Succeeding at Work*. A & C Black Publishers Ltd.

Belbin, R. M. 2010a. *Management Teams: Why They Succeed or Fail*. Routledge.

Belbin, R. M. 2010b. *Team Roles at Work*. Routledge.

Binney, G. et al. 2012. *Living Leadership*. Pearson FT series.

Brent, M. & Dent, F. E. 2010. *The Leader's Guide to Influence: How to Use Soft Skills to Get Hard Results*. Pearson.

Brent, M. & Dent, F. E. 2014. *The Leader's Guide to Managing People: How to Use Soft Skills to Get Hard Results*. Pearson.

Brent, M. & Dent, F. E. 2015. *The Leader's Guide to Coaching & Mentoring: How to Use Soft Skills to Get Hard Results*. Pearson Education.

Brent, M. & McKergow, M. 2010. *No More Heroes*. Coaching at Work.

Bridges, W. 2009. *Managing Transitions: Making the Most of Change*. Nicholas Brealey Publishing.

Bushe, G. 2010. *Clear Leadership: Sustaining Real Collaboration and Partnership at Work*. Davies-Black.

Calne, D. 2000. *Within Reason: Rationality and Human Behavior*. Vintage Books.

Chartered Institute of Personal Development (CIPD). 2011. *The Coaching Climate.*

Chartered Institute of Personal and Development (CIPD). 2013. *Learning and Talent Development Annual Survey.*

Cialdini, R. 2009. *The Psychology of Persuasion*. Collins Business Essentials.

Collins English Dictionary. 2011. Harper Collins, 11th edition.

Corporate Executive Board. 2009.

Covey, S. 2004. *The 7 Habits of Highly Effective People: Powerful Lessons in Personal Change*. Simon & Schuster.

Deloitte University Press. 2016. *Global Human Capital Trends 2016*, http://www2.deloitte.com/US/en/pages/human-capital/articles/introduction-human-capital-trends.htm (accessed 8 November 2016).

Dent, F., Rabbetts, J. & Holton, V. 2013. *The Ashridge Management Index*. Ashridge Business School.

DeRond, M. 2012. *There Is an I in Team: What Elite Athletes and Coaches Really Know about High Performance*. Harvard Business Publishing.

Edmondson, A. 2012. *Teaming: How Organisations Learn, Innovate and Compete in the Knowledge Economy*. Jossey Bass.

Ferguson, A. 2011. *The Independent*, 30 April 2011.

Fleming, K. 2016. *The Leader's Guide to Emotional Agility: How to Use Soft Skills to Get Hard Results*. Pearson.

Fredrickson, B. & Losada, M. 2005. Positive Affect and the Complex Dynamics of Human Flourishing. *American Psychologist* 60(7): 7.

French, J. & Raven, B. 1959. The Bases of Social Power. *Studies in Social Power* 150–167.

Goleman, D. 1996. *Emotional Intelligence*. Bloomsbury.

Goleman, D. 2004. *Working with Emotional Intelligence*. Bloomsbury.

Gratton, L. & Scott, A. 2016. *The 100 Year Life: Living and Working in an Age of Longevity*. Bloomsbury.

Greenleaf, R. K. 1970. *The Servant as Leader*. The Centre For Servant Leadership.

Greenleaf, R. K. & Spears, L. C. 2002. *Servant Leadership*. Paulist Press.

Grint, K. 2005. *Leadership- Limits and Possibilities*. Palgrave Macmillan.

Hargie, O. & Dickson, D. 2004. *Skilled Interpersonal Communication*. Routledge.

Haslam, S. A., Reicher, S. D. & Platow, M. J. 2011. *The New Psychology of Leadership*. Psychology Press.

Hawkins, P. 2014. *Leadership Team Coaching in Practice*. Kogan Page.

Hay Group. 2014. *Building the New Leader: Leadership Challenges of the Future Revealed*. Hay Group.

Honore, S. & Paine Schofield, C. 2012. *Culture Shock: Generation Y and Their Managers Round the World*. Ashridge Business School.

Hornstein, H., Luss, R., & Parker, O. 2002. The Watson Wyatt Human Capital Index And Company Performance: A Definite Impact on Shareholder Wealth. A paper presented at the International Management Conference, Society for Advancement of Management, McLean, Virginia

Katzenbach, J. & Smith, D. 1993. *The Wisdom of Teams: Creating the High-Performance Organisation*. Harvard Business Press.

Lakoff, G. 2009. *The Political Mind: A Cognitive Scientist's Guide to Your Brain and Its' Politics*. Penguin.

Lakoff, G. & Johnson, M. 2008. *Metaphors We Live By*. Chicago University Press.

Lencioni, P. 2002. *The Five Dysfunctions of a Team: A Leadership Fable*. John Wiley & Sons.

Levesque, R. 2015. *Ask*. Dunham Books.

Lowther, M. 2016. Interview with author.

Maister, D., Green, C. & Galford, R. 2002. *The Trusted Advisor*. Simon & Schuster.

Margerison, C. & McCann, D. 2000. *Team Management: Practical New Approaches*. Management Books.

McCall Jr., M. W. 1998. *High Flyers*. HBS Press.

McKergow, M. 2009. Leader as Host, Host as Leader. *International Journal of Leadership in Public Service.*

McKergow, M. 2015. Developing Authentic Leadership - be a Good Host Approaching Leadership in a New Way using the Familiar Techniques of Hosting. *Strategic HR Review*, emaraldinsight.com

McKergow, M. & Bailey, H. 2014. *Host: Six New Roles of Engagement*. Solution Books

Meharabian, A. 2007. *Non Verbal Communication*. Aldine Transaction.

Melville, N. 2015. Personal conversation with authors.

Meuller, J. S. 2012. Why Individuals in Larger Teams Perform Worse. *Organisational Behaviour and Human Decision Processes* 117(1): 111–124.

Parks, S. D. 2005. *Leadership Can Be Taught*. HBR Press.

Porter, E. H. 1996. *Strength Deployment Inventory*. Personal Strengths Publishing Inc.

Reina, D. & Reina, M. 1973. *Trust and Betrayal in the Workplace*. Berrett & Koehler

Reina, D & Reina, M. 2015. *Trust and Betrayal in the Workplace*. Berrett-Koehler.

Rittel, H. & Weber, M. 1973. Dilemmas in a General Theory of Planning. *Policy Sciences* 4: 155–169.

Roberts, K. 2005. *Lovemarks – The Future Beyond Brands*. PowerHouse Books.

Robertson, B. J. 2015. *Holocracy: The Revolutionary Management System That Abolishes Hierarchy*. Penguin.

Royal College of Surgeons. 2014. *The High Performing Surgical Team: A Guide to Best Practice.*

Sanders, R. E. & Fitch, K. L. 2001. The Actual Practise of Compliance Seeking. *Communication Theory*. 11

Schutz, W. 1958. *FIRO: A Three-Dimensional Theory of Interpersonal Behaviour*. New York: Rinehart.

Schwarz, T. & McCarthy, C. 2016. *The Way We're Working Isn't Working*. Simon & Schuster.

Souness, G. 2015. Article in *Sunday Times*, 18 January 2015.

Tuckman, B. W. & Jensen, M. A. C. 1977. Stages of Small Group Development Revisited. *Group and Organisational Studies* 2: 419–427.

Turner, M. 1996. *The Literary Mind*. Oxford University Press.

Watson Wyatt. 2002. *The Human Capital Index Study*, http://www.watsonwyatt.com/hci.

Wheately, M. & Frieze, D. 2011. From Hero to Host. *Resurgence* 264: 14–17.

Whitmore, J. 2010. *Coaching for Performance: GROWing Human Potential and Purpose: The Principles and Practice of Coaching & Leadership*. Nicolas Brealey Publishing.

INDEX